# THE INTERNET IS
# A PLAYGROUND

ISBN 978-0-9886895-0-3
The Internet is a Playground

www.27bslash6.com

### By the same author:

**The Internet is a Playground**
You're holding it.

**I'll Go Home Then; It's Warm and Has Chairs**
The second collection of all new essays and emails.

**Look Evelyn, Duck Dynasty Wiper Blades, We Should Get Them**
The third collection of new essays and emails.

**That's Not How You Wash a Squirrel**
The fourth collection of new essays and emails.

**Wrap It In a Bit of Cheese Like You're Tricking the Dog**
The fifth collection of new essays and emails.

**Walk It Off, Princess**
The sixth collection of new essays and emails.

OFFICE MEMO PRESS

For Seb and Holly. <3

**Free Telescope.**

This page, when rolled into a tube,
makes a telescope with 1:1
magnification.

# Reviews

★☆☆☆☆ "I'm getting your website banned as we speak."
*Lucius Thaller*

★☆☆☆☆ "Sad. I gave you an opportunity to be part of something world changing but you didn't have the vision."
*Simon Edhouse*

★☆☆☆☆ "You're just not that funny. I'm a lot funnier than you. And a better writer. I just haven't written any of the funny stuff I think of down because I don't have time."
*Simon Dempsey*

★☆☆☆☆ "I spoke to a lawyer and he told me I could sue you for defamation. I won't but I could. Keep that in mind."
*Thomas DeMasi*

★☆☆☆☆ "You can put me in your book as long as you change my name and don't use the photo of me eating an orange."
*Shannon Walkley*

★☆☆☆☆ "I've never had head lice."
*Mark Pierce*

★☆☆☆☆ "I made you cabbage soup for lunch, Thomas."
*Lillian Eskander*

# Contents

# Introduction

Thank you for purchasing this book. I apologise in advance for the fact that it contains almost no robots or explosions or exploding robots. If you specifically bought this book for the robot and explosion components, you'll find mention of robots on pages 9, 125, 165, 183, 237, and 241. The only mention of an explosion is on page 183.

My favourite bit of the book is where Richard and Emmeline are shipwrecked on a tropical island and without either the guidance or restrictions of society, emotional feelings and physical changes arise as they reach puberty and fall in love. Later, on page 144, where Richard moves with his mother to a neighbourhood in the San Fernando Valley region of Los Angeles, their new apartment's handyman, an eccentric but kindly Okinawan immigrant, teaches Richard not only martial arts, but also important life lessons such as balancing on a boat.

I used to spend many hours writing stupid posts, mainly to annoy people on social networking sites, but I was constantly finding myself banned. Some moderators have a sense of humour and take on the role of guide among collaborators, others see themselves as teachers among children and, charged with the godlike power of single click censorship, smite those colouring outside the lines. The 27b/6 website was created simply as a site where the content couldn't be touched by moderators and took only a few hits per day. After posting an article concerning paying for an outstanding chiropractors bill with a bad drawing of a spider, the website effectively went viral and received millions of hits per day..

The title of the website, 27b/6, is a vague reference to Orwell's novel Nineteen Eighty Four - which he wrote while living in 27B on floor 6 of his apartment building. Although my nonsense isn't a statement as grand as Orwell's, the site could be seen as an outlet for dealing with my own minor Orwellian nightmares. I don't have caged rats attempting to gnaw their way through my face, but working in the design industry is pretty much the same thing. I tend to create most of my content when I am bored or procrastinating - I started writing as a distraction to working in the design industry, which one might assume is a creative field but is actually not unlike any other form of cubicle prostitution. People often misconstrue apathy for humour. I was called, "An idiot with an occasional vague point" once in a magazine, which I quite liked.

Also, to answer the question I'm most often asked, the email articles in this collection are verbatim. Having said that, I do on occasion change names unless the person has overly annoyed me. I also fix my spelling errors, as is my prerogative, and bad grammar prior to posting. The characters in the non-email articles are people who have annoyed me, work colleagues, and friends.

Regards, David

# Overdue Account

*I read recently of a 'qualified' chiropractor that has been using distance healing for quite some time, claiming he can heal you from his living room. There's no need to visit his office, just call or write and he will do the rest. Apparently he discovered his special chiropractic skill while he was in his car, his foot hurt and he told it to realign itself.*

**From:** Jane Gilles
**Date:** Wednesday 8 Oct 2008 12.19pm
**To:** David Thorne
**Subject:** Overdue account

Dear David,

Our records indicate that your account is overdue by the amount of $233.95. If you have already made this payment please contact us within the next 7 days to confirm payment has been applied to your account and is no longer outstanding.

Yours sincerely, Jane Gilles

From: David Thorne
Date: Wednesday 8 Oct 2008 12.37pm
To: Jane Gilles
Subject: Re: Overdue account

Dear Jane,
I do not have any money so am sending you this drawing I did of a spider instead. I value the drawing at $233.95 so trust that this settles the matter.

Regards, David

From: Jane Gilles
Date: Thursday 9 Oct 2008 10.07am
To: David Thorne
Subject: Re: Re: Overdue account

Dear David,

Thank you for contacting us. Unfortunately we are unable to accept drawings as payment and your account remains in arrears. Please contact us within the next 7 days to confirm payment has been applied to your account and is no longer outstanding.

Yours sincerely, Jane Gilles

**From**: David Thorne
**Date**: Thursday 9 Oct 2008 10.32am
**To**: Jane Gilles
**Subject**: Re: Re: Re: Overdue account

Dear Jane,

Can I have my drawing of a spider back then please?

Regards, David

................................................................................

**From**: Jane Gilles
**Date**: Thursday 9 Oct 2008 11.42am
**To**: David Thorne
**Subject**: Re: Re: Re: Re: Overdue account

Dear David,

You emailed the drawing to me. Do you want me to email it back to you?

Yours sincerely, Jane Gilles

................................................................................

**From**: David Thorne
**Date**: Thursday 9 Oct 2008 11.56am
**To**: Jane Gilles
**Subject**: Re: Re: Re: Re: Re: Overdue account

Dear Jane,

Yes please.

Regards, David

**From:** Jane Gilles
**Date:** Thursday 9 Oct 2008 12.14pm
**To:** David Thorne
**Subject:** Re: Re: Re: Re: Re: Re: Overdue account

Attached <spider.gif>

---

**From:** David Thorne
**Date:** Friday 10 Oct 2008 09.22am
**To:** Jane Gilles
**Subject:** Whose spider is that?

Dear Jane,

Are you sure this drawing of a spider is the one I sent you?

This spider only has seven legs and I do not feel I would have made such an elementary mistake when I drew it.

Regards, David

**From:** Jane Gilles
**Date:** Friday 10 Oct 2008 11.03am
**To:** David Thorne
**Subject:** Re: Whose spider is that?

Dear David,

Yes it is the same drawing. I copied and pasted it from the email you sent me on the 8th.

David your account is still overdue by the amount of $233.95. Please make this payment as soon as possible.

Yours sincerely, Jane Gilles

................................................................................................

**From:** David Thorne
**Date:** Friday 10 Oct 2008 11.05am
**To:** Jane Gilles
**Subject:** Automated Out of Office Response

Thank you for contacting me. I am currently away on leave, travelling through time, and will be returning last week.

Regards, David

................................................................................................

**From:** David Thorne
**Date:** Friday 10 Oct 2008 11.08am
**To:** Jane Gilles
**Subject:** Re: Re: Whose spider is that?

Hello, I am back and have read through your emails and accept that despite missing a leg, that drawing of a spider may indeed be the one I sent you. I realise with hindsight that it is possible you rejected the drawing of a spider due to this obvious limb omission but did not point it out in an effort to avoid hurting my feelings.

As such, I am sending you a revised drawing with the correct number of legs as full payment for any amount outstanding. I trust this will bring the matter to a conclusion.

Regards, David.

From: Jane Gilles
Date: Monday 13 Oct 2008 2.51pm
To: David Thorne
Subject: Re: Re: Re: Whose spider is that?

Dear David,

As I have stated, we do not accept drawings in lieu of money for accounts outstanding. We accept credit cards, cheques, bank cheques, money orders and cash.

Please make a payment this week to avoid incurring any additional fees.

Yours sincerely, Jane Gilles

**From**: David Thorne
**Date**: Monday 13 Oct 2008 3.17pm
**To**: Jane Gilles
**Subject**: Re: Re: Re: Re: Whose spider is that?

I understand and will definitely make a payment this week if I remember. As you have not accepted my second drawing as payment, please return the drawing to me as soon as possible. It was silly of me to assume I could provide you with something of completely no value whatsoever, waste your time and then attach such a large amount to it.

Regards, David.

........................................................................................................

**From**: Jane Gilles
**Date**: Tuesday 14 Oct 2008 11.18am
**To**: David Thorne
**Subject**: Re: Re: Re: Re: Re: Whose spider is that?

Attached <spider2.gif>

# Hello, my name is Shannon and I eat like a snake.

*Due to an extendable jaw and highly acidic saliva levels, I have found that consuming an orange whole and digesting it over the space of many hours, requires almost no effort at all.*

I once ate a rockmelon but of course that took many days to digest. People sometimes assume when they see a hint of orange in my mouth that I am wearing a fashionable form of braces or afflicted with a medical condition requiring me to wear a mouthguard at all times, possibly in case of falling over during a seizure or maybe even that sleeping illness you see in movies sometimes.

Of course I cannot move or do anything while I am digesting but this has not affected my work as I can still move my eyes, allowing me to look out the window and keep an eye on the petty cash tin.

# Simon's Pie Charts

I quite like Simon Edhouse, he's like the school teacher that would pull you aside after class and list, for an hour, every bad aspect of your personality and why you will never get anywhere while you nod and pretend to listen while thinking about how tight Sally Watts jeans were that day and wishing you were at home playing Choplifter on the family's new Amstrad.

I worked with Simon for a while at a branding agency named de Masi Jones. He was employed, as a business development manager, to bring in new clients yet somehow managed to be there for several months without bringing in a single one before leaving to pursue his own projects.

The lack of new clients may possibly be attributed to his being too occupied writing angry emails to other de Masi jones employees such as, "When I worked at Olgilvy in Hong Kong, everyone called me Mr Edhouse and said that I was doing a great job. Not once did the secretary there call me a wanker or have her grotty old g-strings poking out the top of her fat arse everyday making me feel ill." which I found much more entertaining than having to do the work new clients would have entailed.

**From**: Simon Edhouse
**Date**: Monday 16 November 2009 2.19pm
**To**: David Thorne
**Subject**: Logo Design

Hello David,

I would like to catch up as I am working on a really exciting project at the moment and need a logo designed. Basically something representing peer to peer networking.
I have to have something to show prospective clients this week so would you be able to pull something together in the next few days? I will also need a couple of pie charts done for a 1 page website. If deal goes ahead there will be some good money in it for you.

Simon

..........................................................................................

**From**: David Thorne
**Date**: Monday 16 November 2009 3.52pm
**To**: Simon Edhouse
**Subject**: Re: Logo Design

Dear Simon,

Disregarding the fact that you have still not paid me for work I completed earlier this year - despite several assertions that you would do so, I would be delighted to spend my free time creating logos and pie charts for you based on further vague promises of future possible payment. Please find attached pie chart as requested and let me know of any changes required.

Regards, David

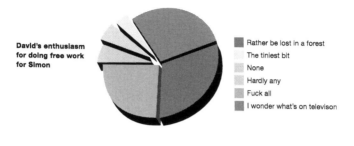

David's enthusiasm
for doing free work
for Simon

- Rather be lost in a forest
- The tiniest bit
- None
- Hardly any
- Fuck all
- I wonder what's on televison

........................................................................................................

**From:** Simon Edhouse
**Date:** Monday 16 November 2009 4.11pm
**To:** David Thorne
**Subject:** Re: Re: Logo Design

Is that supposed to be a fucking joke? I told you the previous projects did not go ahead. I invested a lot more time and energy in those projects than you did. If you put as much energy into the projects as you do being a dickhead you would be a lot more successful.

........................................................................................................

**From:** David Thorne
**Date:** Monday 16 November 2009 5.27pm
**To:** Simon Edhouse
**Subject:** Re: Re: Re: Logo Design

Dear Simon,

You are correct and I apologise. Your last project was actually both commercially viable and original. Unfortunately the part that was commercially viable was not original, and the part that was original was not commercially viable.

I would no doubt find your ideas more 'cutting edge' and original if I had travelled forward in time from the 1950s but, as it stands, your ideas for technology based projects that have already been put into application by other people several years before you thought of them fail to generate the enthusiasm they possibly deserve. Having said that though, if I had travelled forward in time, my time machine would probably put your peer to peer networking technology to shame as not only would it have commercial viability, but also an awesome logo and accompanying pie charts.

Regardless, I have, as requested, attached a logo that represents not only the peer to peer networking project you are currently working on, but working with you in general.

Regards, David

**From:** Simon Edhouse
**Date:** Tuesday 17 November 2009 11.07am
**To:** David Thorne
**Subject:** Re: Re: Re: Re: Logo Design

You just crossed the line. You have no idea about the potential this project has.

The technology allows users to network peer to peer, add contacts, share information and is potentially worth many millions of dollars and your short sightedness just cost you any chance of being involved.

........................................................................................................

**From:** David Thorne
**Date:** Tuesday 17 November 2009 1.36pm
**To:** Simon Edhouse
**Subject:** Re: Re: Re: Re: Re: Logo Design

Dear Simon,

So you have invented Twitter. Congratulations. This is where that time machine would definitely have come in quite handy. When I was about twelve, I read that time slows down when approaching the speed of light so I constructed a time machine by securing my father's portable generator to the back of my mini-bike with rope and attaching the drive belt to the back wheel. Unfortunately, instead of travelling through time and finding myself in the future, I travelled about fifty metres along the footpath at 200mph before finding myself in a bush. When asked by the nurse filling out the hospital accident report "Cause of accident?" I stated 'time travel attempt' but she wrote down 'stupidity'.

If I did have a working time machine, the first thing I would do is go back four days and tell myself to read the warning on the hair removal cream packaging where it recommends not using on sensitive areas. I would then travel several months back to warn myself against agreeing to do copious amounts of design work for an old man wielding the business plan equivalent of a retarded child poking itself in the eye with a spoon, before finally travelling back to 1982 and explaining to myself the long term photographic repercussions of going to the hairdresser and asking for a haircut exactly like Simon LeBon's the day before a large family gathering.

Regards, David

......................................................................................................

**From**: Simon Edhouse
**Date**: Tuesday 17 November 2009 3.29pm
**To**: David Thorne
**Subject**: Re: Re: Re: Re: Re: Logo Design

You really are a fucking idiot. The project I am working on will be more successful than twitter within a year. When I sell the project for 40 million dollars I will ignore any emails from you begging to be a part of it and will send you a postcard from my yaght.

Ciao

**From:** David Thorne
**Date:** Tuesday 17 November 2009 3.58pm
**To:** Simon Edhouse
**Subject:** Re: Re: Re: Re: Re: Re: Re: Logo Design

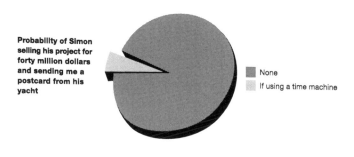

........................................................................................

**From:** Simon Edhouse
**Date:** Tuesday 17 November 2009 4.10pm
**To:** David Thorne
**Subject:** Re: Re: Re: Re: Re: Re: Re: Re: Logo Design

Anyone else would be able to see the opportunity I am presenting but not you. You have to be a fucking smartarse about it.

All I was asking for was a logo and a few piecharts which would have taken you a few fucking hours.

From: David Thorne
Date: Tuesday 17 November 2009 4.25pm
To: Simon Edhouse
Subject: Re: Re: Re: Re: Re: Re: Re: Re: Re: Logo Design

Dear Simon,

Actually, you were asking me to design a logotype which would have taken me a few hours and fifteen years experience. For free. With pie charts.

Usually when people don't ask me to design them a logo, pie charts or website, I, in return, do not ask them to paint my apartment, drive me to the airport, represent me in court or whatever it is they do for a living. Unfortunately though, as your business model consists entirely of "Facebook is cool, I am going to make a website just like that", this non exchange of free services has no foundation as you offer nothing of which I wont ask for.

Regards, David

......................................................................................................

From: Simon Edhouse
Date: Tuesday 17 November 2009 4.43pm
To: David Thorne
Subject: Re: Re: Re: Re: Re: Re: Re: Re: Re: Re: Logo Design

What the fuck is your point? Are you going to do the logo and charts for me or not?

**From:** David Thorne
**Date:** Tuesday 17 November 2009 5.02pm
**To:** Simon Edhouse
**Subject:** Re: Re: Re: Re: Re: Re: Re: Re: Re: Re: Re: Logo Design

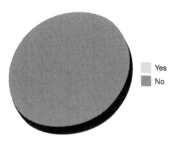

Yes
No

..........................................................................................

**From:** Simon Edhouse
**Date:** Tuesday 17 November 2009 5.13pm
**To:** David Thorne
**Subject:** Re: Re: Re: Re: Re: Re: Re: Re: Re: Re: Re: Re: Logo Design

Don't ever email me again.

**From:** David Thorne
**Date:** Tuesday 17 November 2009 5.19pm
**To:** Simon Edhouse
**Subject:** Re: Re: Re: Re: Re: Re: Re: Re: Re: Re: Re: Re: Re: Logo Design

Okay. Good luck with your project. If you need anything let me know.

Regards, David

...........................................................................................

**From:** Simon Edhouse
**Date:** Tuesday 17 November 2009 5.27pm
**To:** David Thorne
**Subject:** Re: Re: Re: Re: Re: Re: Re: Re: Re: Re: Re: Re: Re: Re: Logo Design

Get fucked.

# Obviously a Foggot

*Sometimes people email me to tell me how their day is going, other times they email me to tell me that I am a dickhead and my website is stupid, which I am already aware of due to many preceding emails stating the same thing.*

*I don't harbor behind a fake name and my email address is clearly listed so it's a simple process for people like George to express their opinion to me but, as I never initiate an email correspondence, simply reply, I'm not always sure why they bother.*

*If I was hetroflexible, I'm pretty sure I would already be aware of the fact and if I'm not, stating that I am is in error so either way it's a pointless exercise. I don't email random people telling them that they have a pet cat named Charles on the off chance they do and are not aware of it.*

**From:** George Lewis
**Date:** Thursday 2 September 2010 6.51pm
**To:** David Thorne
**Subject:** No Subject

I have read your website and it is obviously that your a foggot.

**From:** David Thorne
**Date:** Thursday 2 September 2010 8.07pm
**To:** George Lewis
**Subject:** Re: No Subject

Dear George,

Thank you for your email. While I have no idea what a foggot is, I will assume it is a term of endearment and appreciate you taking time out from calculating launch trajectories or removing temporal lobe tumors to contact me with such. I have attached a signed photo as per your request.

Regards, David

**From:** George Lewis
**Date:** Thursday 2 September 2010 8.49pm
**To:** David Thorne
**Subject:** Re: Re: No Subject

I didnt ask for a photo fag. and I meant faggot you homo so you can shove your signed photo up your ass. You would probably enjoy that. LOL!!!! Go suck your boyfriends dick in a gay club.

......................................................................................................

**From:** David Thorne
**Date:** Thursday 2 September 2010 9.17pm
**To:** George Lewis
**Subject:** Re: Re: Re: No Subject

Dear George,

While I do not have a boyfriend, I do have a friend who is homosexual and I once asked him, "Do you ever think about having sex with me because you are gay?" to which he replied "Do you ever think about having sex with Rosie O'Donnell because you are straight? Same thing."

If I *were* inclined to have a boyfriend, I would select one my height and weight to save having to readjust the driver's seat position. I'm not interested in doubling my wardrobe as I wear the same outfit everyday to facilitate speedy identification should I ever be in a boating accident.

Although I have never been to a gay club as such, when I was about ten, a friend and I constructed a clubhouse in my backyard using timber stolen from a building site down the street. Our club, which we named 'The Kiss Club' due to a certain band being popular at the time, employed an intensive entry exam in which the applicant had to know all the words to

*Love Gun* and not be a girl. Specifically, not my sister. The next day after school, having managed to recruit several new members by promising laminated membership cards and changing the entry exam to 'knowing the names of the band members', we all rode to my place to participate in our first club meeting only to discover my sister, outraged by the 'no girls' rule and armed with a can of paint left over from a recent bedroom redesign, had painted the clubhouse pink and added 'ing' to the end of the word 'Kiss'.

Also, despite your inference, I have managed, up to this point, to avoid putting most things in my bottom. Primarily due to the possibility that I might enjoy it, get carried away, and move on to watermelons or midsize family autos. When I was about eight, I drew a face on my hand and practiced kissing it, which I will admit is a little gay, and I have often thought there would be advantages to homosexuality such as Abercrombie & Fitch reward points, successful couch fabric selection capabilities and the gift of dance. With or without a top on. This would come in extremely useful if I needed five hundred dollars and saw a poster advertising a dance competition with a first prize of five hundred dollars.

Regards, David

..........................................................................................

**From:** George Lewis
**Date:** Thursday 2 September 2010 9.33pm
**To:** David Thorne
**Subject:** Re: Re: Re: Re: No Subject

If you livd close by gaycunt I would be over your place with 5 friends tonight.

**From:** David Thorne
**Date:** Thursday 2 September 2010 10.08pm
**To:** George Lewis
**Subject:** Re: Re: Re: Re: Re: No Subject

Dear George,

I knew we would get along. We've only known each other for one day and already you're organising a party. I am not sure where Gaycunt is but if I did "livd close by" to it, I would definitely be up for that.

We could all sit outside on banana lounges discussing the best way to rebuild a 4WD transmission and agree, through shared stories of conquests supporting our assertions, that there is no basis to the proposition that those least assured of their persuasions are the first to condemn others for theirs. Although the ideal would be for everyone to be capable of love without fear, restraint, or obligation, clearly this does not apply to homosexuals.

At no time during the night would you comment on how much you liked my Abercrombie & Fitch pants or ask, "is that a Marcel Breuer couch? I love the fabric selection," and when we danced, we would all leave our tops on.

Regards, David

..........................................................................................................

**From:** George Lewis
**Date:** Friday 3 September 2010 1.18pm
**To:** David Thorne
**Subject:** Re: Re: Re: Re: Re: Re: No Subject

no fag I live in Charleston west virginia the best country in the world. I wasnt sying it would be a party. we would smash your fucking skull in and if your calling me a fag you can get fucked becasue I have a girlfriend.

........................................................................................

**From:** David Thorne
**Date:** Friday 3 September 2010 1.56pm
**To:** George Lewis
**Subject:** Yeehaw y'all

Dear George,

Is she also your sister? I checked her photos on your Facebook page and while she's not exactly my type, I accept that other people have different preferences. Even when those preferences include facial tattoos and stretch pants constructed from sufficient material to shelter a small village. And their livestock.

Some men enjoy dancing with other men without their tops on while others prefer the company of a woman two KFC family buckets away from upsetting the planet's rotational axis.

I read somewhere that Eskimos prefer women of girth as it provides warmth at night. I have seen the size of those igloos though and there is no way your girlfriend would make it through the opening. You could probably just construct one around her and despite the hassle of having to trudge out into the snow every day to catch and prepare the eighty seals required to maintain her mass, it would be like a kiln in there. If I were an ́Eskimo, I would build my igloo next to a supermarket or on a tropical beach.

Regards, David

**From:** George Lewis
**Date:** Friday 3 September 2010 2.01pm
**To:** David Thorne
**Subject:** Re: Yeehaw y'all

She isnt fat you fag. and that she got that tattoo is a teardrop becasue her family is dead.

---

**From:** David Thorne
**Date:** Friday 3 September 2010 2.06pm
**To:** George Lewis
**Subject:** Re: Re: Yeehaw y'all

Did she eat them?

---

**From:** George Lewis
**Date:** Friday 3 September 2010 2.32pm
**To:** David Thorne
**Subject:** Re: Re: Re: Yeehaw y'all

Get fucked fag her family they died in a crash. have some respect. Go put some more gel in your hair and dye it balck like a emo skinny fag. And how can you see my facebook page pictures?

**From:** David Thorne
**Date:** Friday 3 September 2010 3.02pm
**To:** George Lewis
**Subject:** Re: Re: Re: Re: Yeehaw y'all

Dear George,

Yes, I have heard those motorhomes can be a bitch to steer. Especially around tight corners during a police chase or moonshine run.

I will concede to half of your description of me as a "skinny fag" being correct. If our bodies are temples, mine would be a heavily shelled Iranian mosque. To rectify this, I have instigated a fitness and weight training regimen. Once a week I carry two heavy garbage bags out to the sidewalk and jog back. As this week was my first session and I did not want to over exert myself, I took the car. Obviously with a few breaks in between to re-hydrate and stretch.

Although hardly an emo, I understand their pain. If I looked in the mirror and saw an anorexic version of Pugsly Adams staring back at me I would probably start cutting myself as well. I will admit to having dyed my hair once though. The product, misrepresented as 'Natural Black' instead of 'Astro Boy black', turned my hair as dark as an adequate simile describing just how black it actually was and stained my forehead and ears purple. In an attempt to blend the colour, I rubbed the remainder of the mixture onto my face, figuring it might look like a tan. I spent the following two weeks telling people that I could not leave the house due to agoraphobia, an illness usually self-diagnosed by the unemployed as an excuse to stay home and masturbate or play Wii.

I have access to your Facebook page due to the friend request you accepted from the Oscar Wilde profile I constructed yesterday. I assumed the name would hold no relevance to you and, consistency being the last refuge of the unimaginative, I typed 'Redneck wearing baseball cap' into Google Images to locate a photo you would identify and feel comfortable with.

Regards, David

---

**From:** George Lewis
**Date:** Friday 3 September 2010 4.48pm
**To:** David Thorne
**Subject:** Re: Re: Re: Re: Re: Yeehaw y'all

Thats fraud. I will report you to the police and to facebook fag. i would shoot you in the face with my 308 if you were here right now.

---

**From:** David Thorne
**Date:** Friday 3 September 2010 5.19pm
**To:** George Lewis
**Subject:** tarded

Dear George,

Yes, I'm fairly certain there is a worldwide criminal investigation network dedicated solely to bringing those who construct fake Facebook profiles to justice. I believe the punishment is tar and feathering in most parts of the world except West Virginia where you are stripped naked, oiled up and chased around a paddock while wearing a pig mask. Apparently in West Virginia, this is also known as a 'date'.

Variations include substituting the paddock with a motorhome or the person with an actual pig. Or in your case, both.

Also, as it is probably far more acceptable for men in West Virginia to hold guns than hands, I will assume the term 'shooting me in the face with your 308' is not a euphemism.

Regards, David

---

**From:** George Lewis
**Date:** Friday 3 September 2010 7.04pm
**To:** David Thorne
**Subject:** Re: tarded

Ive deleted you from my facebook and reported you. i hope you die of aids fag. Dont bothering emailing me again becasue I wont read it.

---

**From:** David Thorne
**Date:** Friday 3 September 2010 7.12pm
**To:** George Lewis
**Subject:** dneck

Yes you will.

---

**From:** George Lewis
**Date:** Friday 3 September 2010 7.16pm
**To:** David Thorne
**Subject:** Re: dneck

No I fucking wont fag

# Simon's Good Ideas for Websites

*Hello, my name is Simon and I have good ideas for websites all the time. Every single one of my ideas would make lots of money. Do not copy these ideas because they are mine.*

### everything.com

This would be a website where instead of having to look all over the internet for what you want, it would all be in the one place. This would effectively end the need for search engines so I would have to be careful that google representatives do not kill me in my sleep.

### whereaboutsami.com

This would be a website where users can write the name of the city and street they are on and I would tell them where they are.

### armbook.com

Similar to facebook but people upload photos of their arms.

### onlinepetfrog.com

Instead of buying their own pet frog, users would pay a fee and I would buy them a frog and look after it. Users could log on anytime to a live webcam and see how their frog is going and send live requests for me to wave the frog's hand at the camera or bang on the glass if it is sleeping.

### amihavingaheartattack.com

A website for people having a heart attack.

### whatkindofcoughisthat.com

A website that contains sound files of different coughs. Each cough would have a description to allow the user to sound match and determine the kind of cough they have before going to the chemist and buying either dry or wet cough medicine.

### yourloungeroom.com

Users of this website would be able take a photo of their lounge room and upload it to the site. Then I would tell them what furniture does not look good.

### howdoigettowhereiam.com

This site would contain a link to the page the user is currently on.

### uploadyourscreen.com

A website where the user takes a screenshot of their computer screen and uploads it so that when they are looking at porn and the boss walks past, they can type in the link and go to it instead.

## whichonetowear.com

Users of this website would take photos of themselves wearing every combination of every article of clothing they own then upload the images to a user database. Every day, instead of trying on clothing, the user can choose an outfit by simply viewing their choices online.

## deceasedlovedones.com

This would be a website where you pay a fee to join and are given your own web page with an empty blog. In the event of your death, you can use the page to write a message to your loved ones. Similar setup to prepaid funerals. Your loved ones can either log on and check whether you have left a message for them or can opt to receive an email notifying them when you leave a message

## everyoneschair.com

A website where you can upload a picture of your chair and then if anyone tries to use your chair and you say, "Thats my chair!" and they ask, "Has it got your name on it?" you can send them a link to your photo of the chair which will have the caption, 'This is (your name)'s chair'.

## screensavingpage.com

A website that is a black page so that people can go there instead of buying a screensaver.

## picturesofpegs.com

This website would contain pictures of pegs, allowing the user to have access to pictures of pegs whenever they need them.

# Lifesize Lucius
# Free Cutout Doll

Sexy time Lucius. Not just sexy underpants, sexy underpants full of luciusness. Like a boy scout, Lucius is always prepared and knows the best way to bait a trap is with love.

Hell's Angel Lucius. He's a bad boy ladies, playing by his own rules and showing an utter lack of respect for authority, apart from the police, road rules and signs

Shower time Lucius. Scrubbing up and shaving down for a big night out. He's fresh fragrant and economical due to a single bar of soap lasting several years.

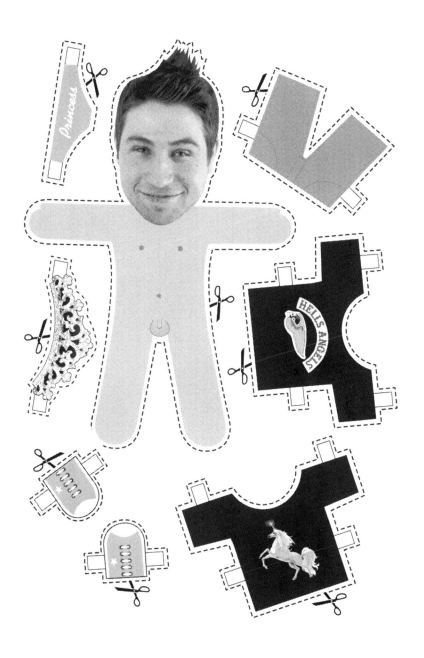

# Matthew's Party

*A few weeks ago, a guy moved into the apartment across from me. I know little about him apart from the fact that he owns cane furniture. Last week, when I checked my mailbox, I found that he had left me a note stating that he was having a party. It was vibrant and had balloons, and I thought, "That's nice, he's having a house-warming party and has sent me an invite."*

*Upon further inspection, I realised it wasn't an invite.*

Hello! My name is Matthew and I have moved into Apartment 3. I m having a house warming party next week on the 14th, if the noise gets to loud that night let me know. Nice to meet you anyhow let me know if you ever need anything. Cheers Matthew

mobile 04█████████
email matthews██████████.au

**From:** David Thorne
**Date:** Monday 8 Dec 2008 11.04am
**To:** Matthew Smythe
**Subject:** R.S.V.P.

Dear Matthew,

Thank you for the party invite. At first glance I thought it may be a child's party what with it being vibrant and having balloons but I realise you probably did your best with what little tools were available. I wouldn't miss it for the world. What time would you like me there?

Regards, David

...............................................................................

**From:** Matthew Smythe
**Date:** Monday 8 Dec 2008 3.48pm
**To:** David Thorne
**Subject:** Re: R.S.V.P.

Hi David

Sorry the note was just to let you know that we might be a bit loud that night. The house warming is really just for friends and family but you can drop past for a beer if you like.

Cheers Matthew

...............................................................................

**From:** David Thorne
**Date:** Monday 8 Dec 2008 5.41pm
**To:** Matthew Smythe
**Subject:** Re: Re: R.S.V.P.

Thanks Matthew,

Including me in your list of friends and family means a lot. You and I don't tend to have long discussions when we meet in the hallway and I plan to put a stop to that. Next time we bump into each other I intend to have a very long conversation with you and I am sure you are looking forward to that as much as I am. I have told my friend Ross that you are having a party and he is as excited as I am. Do you want us to bring anything or will everything be provided?

Regards, David

From: Matthew Smythe
Date: Tuesday 9 Dec 2008 10.01am
To: David Thorne
Subject: Re: Re: Re: R.S.V.P.

Hi David

As I said, my housewarming is just for friends and family. There's not a lot of room so cant really have to many people come. Sorry about that mate.

Cheers Matthew

From: David Thorne
Date: Tuesday 9 Dec 2008 2.36pm
To: Matthew Smythe
Subject: Re: Re: Re: Re: R.S.V.P.

Dear Matthew,

I can appreciate that, our apartments are not very large are they?

I myself like to go for a jog each night but fear leaving the house so I have to jog on the spot taking very small steps with my arms straight down. I understand the problems of space restrictions all too well and, if you'd like to store some of your cane furniture at my place during the party, you are quite welcome to. If we were to put it in my spare room for the night and scatter cushions in your apartment, this would provide a lot more seating and create a cosy atmosphere at the same time. I have a mirror ball that you can borrow.

I told Ross not to invite anyone else due to the space constraints so it will just be us two and my other friend Simon.

When I told Simon that Ross and I were going to a party he became quite angry that I had not invited him as well so I really didn't have any choice as he can become quite violent. Sometimes I'm afraid to even be in the same room as him.

So just myself, Ross and Simon. Simon's girlfriend has a work function on that night but might come along after that if she can get a lift with friends.

Regards, David

..................................................................................

**From:** Matthew Smythe
**Date:** Tuesday 9 Dec 2008 4.19pm
**To:** David Thorne
**Subject:** Re: Re: Re: Re: Re: R.S.V.P.

Wtf? Nobody can come to the houswarming party it is just for friends and family. I dont even know these people. How do you know I have cane furniture? Are you the guy in apartment 1?

**From:** David Thorne
**Date:** Tuesday 9 Dec 2008 6.12pm
**To:** Matthew Smythe
**Subject:** Re: Re: Re: Re: Re: Re: R.S.V.P.

Hi Matthew,

I understand it is an exclusive party and I appreciate you trusting my judgement on who to bring.

I just assumed you have cane furniture, doesn't everybody?

Ross rang me today all excited about the party and asked me what the theme is, I told him that I don't think there is a theme and we discussed it and feel that it should be an eighties themed party. I have a white suit and projector and am coming as Nik Kershaw. I have made a looping tape of 'wouldn't it be good' to play as I am sure you will agree that this song has stood the test of time well.

I'm in the process of redesigning your invites appropriately and will get a few hundred of them printed off later today.

I will have to ask you for the money for this as print cartridges for my Epson are pretty expensive. They stopped making this model a month after I bought it and I have to get the cartridges sent from China. Around $120 should cover it.

You can just pop the money in my letter box if I don't see you before tonight.

Regards, David

**From:** Matthew Smythe
**Date:** Wednesday 10 Dec 2008 11.06pm
**To:** David Thorne
**Subject:** Re: Re: Re: Re: Re: Re: Re: R.S.V.P.

There is no theme for the party it is just a few friends and family. noone else can come IT IS ONLY FOR MY FRIENDS AND FAMILY do you understand? Do not print anything out because I am not paying for something I dont need and didnt ask you to do! look I am sorry but i am heaps busy and that night is not convenient. Are you in apartment 1?

..........................................................................................

**From:** David Thorne
**Date:** Thursday 11 Dec 2008 9.15am
**To:** Matthew Smythe
**Subject:** Re: Re: Re: Re: Re: Re: Re: Re: R.S.V.P.

Hello Matthew,

I agree that it is not very convenient and must admit that when I first received your invitation I was perplexed that it was on a Sunday night but who am I to judge? No, I am in apartment 3B. Our bedroom walls are touching so when we are sleeping our heads are only a few feet apart. If I put my ear to the wall I can hear you.

I also agree with you that having a particular theme for your party may not be the best choice, it makes more sense to leave it open as a generic fancy dress party, that way everyone can come dressed in whatever they want. Once, I went to a party in a bear outfit which worked out well as it was freezing and I was the only one warm. As it won't be cold the night of your party, I have decided to come as a ninja. I think it would be really good if you dressed as a ninja as well and we could perform a martial arts display for the other guests. I have real swords and will bring them.

If you need help with your costume let me know, I have made mine by wrapping a black t-shirt around my face with a hooded jacket and cut finger holes in black socks for the gloves. I do not have any black pants so will spray paint my legs on the night. It is a little hard to breathe in the costume so I will need you to keep the window open during the party to provide good air circulation. Actually, I just had a thought, what if I arrived 'through' the window like a real ninja. We should definitely do that. I just measured the distance between our balconies and I should be able to jump it. I once leapt across a creek that was over five metres wide and almost made it.

Also, you mentioned in your invitation that if there is anything I need, to let you know. My car is going in for a service next week and I was wondering, seeing as we are good friends now, if it would be ok to borrow yours on that day? I hate catching the bus as they are full of poor people who don't own cars.

Regards, David

..................................................................................

From: Matthew Smythe
Date: Thursday 11 Dec 2008 3.02pm
To: David Thorne
Subject: Re: Re: Re: Re: Re: Re: Re: Re: Re: R.S.V.P.

WTF? No you cant borrow my car and there is no fucking 3B. I reckon you are that guy from Apartment 1. You are not coming to my house warming and you are not bringing any of your friends. What the fuck is wrong with you??? The only people invited are friends and family I told you that. It is just drinks there is no fucking fancy dress and only people i know are coming! I dont want to be rude but jesus fucking christ man.

........................................................................................

**From:** David Thorne
**Date:** Sunday 14 Dec 2008 2.04am
**To:** Matthew Smythe
**Subject:** Party

Hello Matthew,

I have been away since Thursday so have not been able to check my email from home. Flying back late today in time for the party and just wanted to say that we are really looking forward to it.

We will probably get there around eleven or twelve, just when it starts to liven up. Simon's girlfriend Cathy's work function was cancelled so she can make it after all which is good news. She will probably have a few friends with her so they will take the minivan.

Also, I have arranged a Piñata.

Regards, David

# LILLBOT3000™

*Introducing the next generation in staff replacement technologies. The LILLBOT3000™ has been designed to replace a Lillian in all required actions, including adoration mode which activates automatically when Master Unit (Thomas) enters the room.*

### Features:

Semi-lifelike appearance.

Budapest Peasant Mode (Cooks cabbage based meal & serves to Master Unit).

Removable head. Replacement heads available.

Ability to speak 4 phrases including, "Your hair looks nice today, Thomas," and, "Do i please you?"

Self lubricating (within 50 metres of Master Unit).

USB and Firewire Ports.

# Tom's Haircut

*Rumours that Thomas takes a photo of Carol Brady to the hairdresser have been proven unfounded. Here is finally conclusive evidence that there are indeed considerable differences between the two haircuts; Tom's hair is darker and Carol's has slightly more body – possibly due to the two using different shampoo and conditioner products – Carol uses Johnson & Johnson brand while Thomas uses the natural oils from his body which Lillian harvests for him using a custom made spatula.*

Photographic Evidence 1

Darker shade, no highlights towards the sides.

Photographic Evidence 2

Carol's hair is a lighter shade with highlights towards the sides.

# Shopping With Simon

*Hello, my name is Simon Dempsey and I love IKEA so much I want to marry it. Can you believe the prices on glass tea light holders? Seventy cents. That is unbelievable. I will get ten.*

*Here is my simple step-by-step guide to buying a sofa from IKEA. Some people may think that purchasing a sofa would be a simple exercise but with determination and a little planning, you can ensure that it is a painful process.*

### Step 1

Ring David at 7.40am and ask him if he will come to IKEA with you. It is important to ring this early as David will be disorientated and agree to anything.

### Step 2

Ring David again at 8.05am to check that he got up as getting to IKEA early is imperative. This twenty-five minute interval will ensure that if David did get up, he will be in the shower when you call. Ring David again at 8.45 to enquire where he is and ask him to get you a large latte on the way. If he declines, tell him not to be a selfish prick and remind him of the time you fed his fish.

## Step 3

When David arrives, inform him that you are taking his car because it is bigger. This is also the time to inform him that you are buying a sofa and he will need to rent a trailer on the way. Now that David is at your place you can get ready at your leisure. As you just put the clothes you want to wear in the dryer, he will have to wait an hour anyway. Make him useful during this time by having him edit a website you are working on about Australian architecture.

## Step 4

On the way to IKEA, complain about David's choice in music. Demand a better selection. Make David pull over and tune his stereo to your ipod's itrip and play eighties dance tracks such as 'Big in Japan' by Alphaville loud enough for cars around you to hear. Sing the chorus. If you get the words wrong, explain that's the way they are in another version.

## Step 5

When you get to IKEA, do not go straight to the sofa section. Follow the path IKEA has set for you to take and stop and look at every item. Point out the price and comparison of each product by cross referencing it with the IKEA catalogue. Remember to stop at each location point and consult the 'you are here' diagram before progressing. Inform David every two minutes of your exact location in the store by marking your journey on the IKEA map with your IKEA pencil.

## Step 6

At the sofa section, sit on every couch and pretend you are watching television. Make David sit next to you like a couple.

Also, whenever David is more than five metres away, call out questions such as, "What is the foam density of that one?" loud enough for a thirty metre radius to hear. Consult with the staff about every couch. Researching sofas on the internet before you go will enable you to discuss frame warp and fabric weave. Asking about colour choices and availability will involve looking through large sample books. Consult David on each swatch.

## Step 7

Once you have made your selection, do not leave the store. Purchase a coffee table and shelf unit and tell David that he will help you put them together when you get home. Also purchase lamps, glass tea light holders, cutlery, ice cube trays, cushions, stackable boxes, an ironing board cover, a quilt cover set and a rug. Make David carry everything, explaining that you need your hands free to write on the IKEA product slip with your IKEA pencil.

## Step 8

Before leaving, inform David that you would like to try the famous Swedish Meatballs at the IKEA restaurant. If he states that he will wait in the car, explain that you are shopping together, not one person shopping and the other waiting in the car. Discuss the meatballs on the drive home.

# Shannon's Blanket of Security

*Due to there being no petty cash left, with which Shannon was planning to buy her lunch, Shannon initiates operation "lunch money" with the unveiling of her new Blanket Of Security System (B.O.S S). The petty cash protection vehicle features Internet access for downloading iTunes and windows for looking out of.*

# PERMISSION SLIP

Dear Parent/Guardian of ___Seb Thorne___

On Monday the 22nd of March, classes from year 5 and 6 will be attending a presentation held outside of school grounds at the Mary Richardson Memorial Hall. During the presentation, the true meaning of Easter will be explained in an entertaining and fun filled play performed by members of the Grange Uniting Church youth drama group. Students must have a signed permission slip prior to departure. If you give your child permission to attend this presentation, please sign and return to the school with your child. If you have any questions about the presentation, please call me on ▓▓▓▓▓▓▓ or send me an email to darr▓▓▓▓▓▓▓▓▓▓▓▓▓▓▓u

Darryl Robinson School Chaplain

☑ I give my child permission
☐ I do not give my child permission

to attend the Mary Richardson Memorial Hall on 22.3.2010 for a class presentation.

_____

Parent / Guardian signature

58

# Permission Slip

*While preaching isn't allowed in Australian public schools, it's apparently fine to replace school counselors with 'Christian Volunteers' such as Darryl. A few years ago, the government realised that they could hand over school counseling roles to a willing Christian church without having to pay for the privilege. Now almost half of Australian public schools have a Christian volunteer as a full time member of the school community with parents having no direct control of how much their children are exposed to.*

*Although usually an advocate of people being entitled to their opinions, sexual preferences and beliefs, I seem to have developed some form of mental glitch that makes me want to punch Darryl's fat head.*


**From:** David Thorne
**Date:** Wednesday 10 March 2010 7.12pm
**To:** Darryl Robinson
**Subject:** Permission Slip

Dear Darryl,

I have received your permission slip featuring what I can only assume is a levitating rabbit about to drop an egg on Jesus.

Thank you for pre-ticking the permission box as this has saved me not only from having to make a choice, but also from having to make my own forty five degree downward stroke followed by a twenty percent longer forty five degree upward stroke. Without your guidance, I may have drawn a picture of a cactus wearing a hat by mistake.

As I trust my offspring's ability to separate fact from fantasy, I am happy for him to participate in your indoctrination process on the proviso that all references to 'Jesus' are replaced with the term 'Purportedly Magic Jew.'

Regards, David

. . . . . . . . . . . . . . . . . . . . . . . . . . . . . . . . . . . . . . . . . . . . . . . . . . . . . . . . . . . . . . . . . . . . . . . . . . . . . . . . . .

**From:** Darryl Robinson
**Date:** Thursday 11 March 2010 9.18am
**To:** David Thorne
**Subject:** Re: Permission Slip

Hello David

The tick in the box already was a mistake I noticed after printing them all. I've seen the play and it's not indoctrinating anyone. It's a fun play performed by a great bunch of kids. You do not have to be religious to enjoy it. You are welcome to attend if you have any concerns.

Darryl Robinson, School Chaplain

**From:** David Thorne
**Date:** Thursday 11 March 2010 11.02am
**To:** Darryl Robinson
**Subject:** Re: Re: Permission Slip

Dear Darryl,

Thank you for the kind offer, being unable to think of anything more exciting than attending your entertaining and fun filled afternoon, I tried harder and thought of about four hundred things.

I was actually in a Bible based play once and played the role of 'Annoyed about having to do this.' My scene involved offering a potted plant, as nobody knew what Myrrh was, to a plastic baby Jesus, then standing between 'I forgot my costume so am wearing the teacher's poncho' and 'I don't feel very well'. Highlights of the play included a nervous donkey with diarrhoea causing 'I don't feel very well' to vomit onto the back of Mary's head, and the lighting system, designed to provide a halo effect around the manger, overheating and setting it alight.

The teacher, later criticised for dousing an electrical fire with a bucket of water and endangering the lives of children, left the building in tears and the audience in silence. We only saw her again briefly when she came to the school to collect her poncho.

Also, your inference that I am without religion is incorrect and I am actually torn between two faiths; while your god's promise of eternal life is quite persuasive, the Papua New Guinean mud god, Pikkiwoki, is promising a pig and as many coconuts as you can carry.

Regards, David

**From:** Darryl Robinson
**Date:** Thursday 11 March 2010 2.52pm
**To:** David Thorne
**Subject:** Re: Re: Re: Permission Slip

Hello David

It would be a pity for Seb to miss out on the important message of hope that the story of the resurrection gives, but if you don't want him to attend the presentation on Monday then just tick the other box.

Darryl Robinson, School Chaplain

........................................................................................

**From:** David Thorne
**Date:** Thursday 11 March 2010 5.09pm
**To:** Darryl Robinson
**Subject:** Re: Re: Re: Re: Permission Slip

Dear Darryl,

I understand the importance the resurrection story holds in your particular religion. If I too knew some guy that had been killed and placed inside a cave with a rock in front of it and I visited the cave to find the rock moved and his body gone, the only logical assumption would be that he had risen from the dead and is the son of God.

Once, my friend Simon was rushed to hospital to have his appendix removed and I visited him the next day to find his bed empty. I immediately sacrificed a goat and burnt a witch in his name but it turned out that he had not had appendicitis, just needed a good poo, and was at home playing Playstation.

I realise Playstation was not around in those days but they probably had the equivalent. A muddy stick or something. I would have said "Can someone please check if Jesus is at home playing with his muddy stick, if not, then and only then should we all assume, logically, that he has risen from the dead and is the son of God."

If we accept though, that Jesus was the son of an Infinite Being capable of anything, he probably did have a Playstation. Probably a Playstation 7. I know I have to get my offspring all the latest gadgets. God would probably have said to him, "I was going to wait another two thousand years to give you this but seeing as you have been good... just don't tell your mother about Grand Theft Auto."

Also, is it true that Jesus can be stabbed during a sword fight and be okay due to the fact that he can only die if he gets his head chopped off?

Regards, David

..........................................................................................................

**From:** Darryl Robinson
**Date:** Friday 12 March 2010 10.13am
**To:** David Thorne
**Subject:** Re: Re: Re: Re: Re: Permission Slip

Nowhere in the Bible does Jesus have a sword fight. Learning the teachings of the Bible is not just about religion. It teaches a set of ethics that are sadly not taught by parents nowadays.

Darryl Robinson, School Chaplain

**From:** David Thorne
**Date:** Friday 12 March 2010 2.23pm
**To:** Darryl Robinson
**Subject:** Re: Re: Re: Re: Re: Re: Permission Slip

Dear Darryl,

You raise a valid point and I appreciate you pointing out my failings as a parent. Practising a system of ethics based on the promise of a reward, in your case an afterlife, is certainly preferable to practising a system of ethics based on it simply being the right thing to do.

Many years ago, I lived next door to a Christian named Mr Stevens. You could tell he was a Christian because he had a fish sticker on his Datsun. He used to wave at us kids from his bathroom window on hot summer days as we played in the sprinkler. I learnt a lot from Mr Stevens. Mainly about wrestling holds. The trick is to oil up really well. I would often lie on his living room rug looking up at the pictures of sunsets behind quotes from Psalms while waiting for him to unwrap his legs from around my torso.

Your job would be made much easier if, after making the school children sit through an hour of church youth group teens dancing, singing and re-enacting Jewish magic tricks, you simply told them that it was just a small taste of what hell is like and if they didn't believe in Jesus they would have to sit through it again.

When I was at school, we were forced to attend a similar presentation. Herded into the gym under the pretence of free chips, we were assaulted with an hour of hippies playing guitars and a dance routine featuring some kind of colourful coat and a lot of looking upwards. Due to the air-conditioning in the packed gym not working and it being a hot day, the hippie wearing the colourful coat blacked out mid performance and struck his head against the front edge of the stage spraying the first row of cross-legged children with blood. Unconscious, he also urinated. There was screaming and an ambulance involved and everyone agreed it was the best play they had ever seen.

Regards, David

....................................................................................

**From:** Darryl Robinson
**Date:** Friday 12 March 2010 2.47pm
**To:** David Thorne
**Subject:** Re: Re: Re: Re: Re: Re: Re: Permission Slip

I don't see what any of that has to do with this play. It's important for children to have balance in their life and spirituality is as important in a childs life as everything else. There's an old saying that life without religion is life without beauty.

Darryl Robinson, School Chaplain

....................................................................................

**From:** David Thorne
**Date:** Friday 12 March 2010 3.36pm
**To:** Darryl Robinson
**Subject:** Re: Re: Re: Re: Re: Re: Re: Re: Permission Slip

Dear Darryl,

I agree completely that balance is an important component of a child's education. I will assume then that you will also be organising a class excursion to a play depicting the fifteen billion year expansion of the universe from its initial particle soup moments following the big bang through to molecule coalescion, galaxy and planetary formation and eventually life?

Perhaps your church youth group could put together an interpretive dance routine representing the behaviour of Saturn's moon Hyperion, shattered by an ancient collision and falling randomly back together, tugged to and fro by the gravitational pull of Titan, sixteen sister moons, the multi-billionfold moonlets of Saturn's rings, Saturn's gravitational field, companion planets, the variability's of Sol, stars, galaxy, neighbouring galaxies... or possibly not; according to an old saying, there is no beauty in this.

Also, while I understand that the play is to be held outside school grounds, due to the fact that it is illegal to present medieval metaphysic propaganda in public schools, it is also my understanding that you are now required by law, as of last year, to go by the title Christian Volunteer rather than School Chaplain. A memo you may have missed or filed in your overflowing 'facts that cease to exist when they are ignored' tray.

Regards, David

......................................................................................

**From:** Darryl Robinson
**Date:** Monday 15 March 2010 9.22am
**To:** David Thorne
**Subject:** Re: Re: Re: Re: Re: Re: Re: Re: Re: Permission Slip

I'm not going to waste any more time replying to your stupid emails. If you don't want your child to attend the play just indicate that on the permission slip.

**From:** David Thorne
**Date:** Monday 15 March 2010 11.04am
**To:** Darryl Robinson
**Subject:** Re: Re: Re: Re: Re: Re: Re: Re: Re: Re: Permission Slip

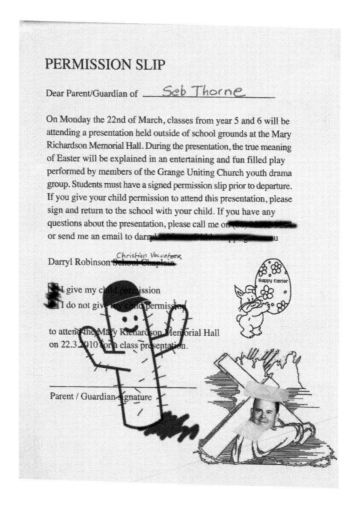

## PERMISSION SLIP

Dear Parent/Guardian of _____ Seb Thorne _____

On Monday the 22nd of March, classes from year 5 and 6 will be attending a presentation held outside of school grounds at the Mary Richardson Memorial Hall. During the presentation, the true meaning of Easter will be explained in an entertaining and fun filled play performed by members of the Grange Uniting Church youth drama group. Students must have a signed permission slip prior to departure. If you give your child permission to attend this presentation, please sign and return to the school with your child. If you have any questions about the presentation, please call me on ▓▓▓▓▓▓▓ or send me an email to darr▓▓▓▓▓▓▓▓▓▓▓▓▓▓u

Darryl Robinson ~~School Chaplain~~ *Christian Volunteer*

☑ I give my child permission
☐ I do not give my child permission

to attend the Mary Richardson Memorial Hall on 22.3.2010 for a class presentation.

Parent / Guardian Signature

Happy Easter

**From:** Darryl Robinson
**Date:** Monday 15 March 2010 2.11pm
**To:** David Thorne
**Subject:** No Subject

I will pray for you.

---

**From:** David Thorne
**Date:** Monday 15 March 2010 2.19pm
**To:** Darryl Robinson
**Subject:** Re: No Subject

Thanks. Mention that I want a Toyota Prado if you get the chance. A white one. With dark grey leather interior and sat nav.

Regards, David

---

**From:** Darryl Robinson
**Date:** Tuesday 16 March 2010 9.20am
**To:** David Thorne
**Subject:** Re: Re: No Subject

I've had enough of your nonsense. Dont email me again.

**From:** GOD
**Date:** Tuesday 16 March 2010 10.18am
**To:** Darryl Robinson
**Subject:** Word of God

DARYL, THIS IS GOD. BUY DAVID A TOYOTA PRADO. A WHITE ONE. WITH DARK GREY LEATHER INTERIOR AND SAT NAV.

...............................................................................................................

**From:** Darryl Robinson
**Date:** Tuesday 16 March 2010 2.35pm
**To:** GOD  Cc: David Thorne
**Subject:** Re: Word of God

I'm serious.

...............................................................................................................

**From:** GOD
**Date:** Tuesday 16 March 2010 2.48pm
**To:** Darryl Robinson
**Subject:** Re: Re: Word of God

OK.

# Bill's Guide to the Internet

*Hello, my name is Bill and welcome to my guide to the Internet. Basically, everything on the Internet is rubbish but I will try to pinpoint the main areas to avoid. The Internet is full of idiots writing rubbish for other idiots to read. If I want to find something out I will ask someone or read a book. I paid over three thousand dollars for my complete leather bound set of Funk & Wagnalls in 1967 and if it is not in there then it is not worth knowing. Also, man will walk on the moon before I have a Facebook page.*

## Google

When I was young and I wanted to know something, I was beaten for being too inquisitive. That's the problem with the young people today; they have a Google answer for everything. If they had to walk to library every time they had something stupid to ask, they would ask a lot less stupid questions.

## Google Images

Google Images is useless. I used it once to search for a photo of farm equipment and it showed me twenty thousand pictures of horse dicks.

## Blogging

I read a blog once by someone who had bought a scarf and he went on for about three hundred paragraphs about his scarf and where he bought it and how it made him feel. The last time I bought a scarf I wore it. End of story. I didn't write a novel about it.

## Chatrooms

If I wanted to chat with strangers, I would pick up the phone and press random numbers. I tried a chatroom once and was talking to guy who claimed he was an obese fifty-three year old man living in a caravan park but there is no way of knowing if these people are telling the truth.

## The Bath Mat

I realise this isn'y Internet related but I can't understand why it is so hard for people to hang the bath mat over the bath when they are finished using it. I don't leave the mat all soggy for other people to walk on after I have been in there.

## Twitter

Why would I want anybody I don't know knowing what I am doing? I don't yell out to everyone in the supermarket "I am buying oranges" so why would I want to do it on my Internet?

## Facebook

I have a photo album on my bookshelf full of faces of people I know which I haven't opened since 1982 so why would I want their faces on my internet?

## Reddit / Digg

These sites are the online equivalent of walking down the street, finding a rock shaped like a frog and holding it up in the air while yelling for all my neighbours to come out and tell me what they think of my frog shaped rock. My neighbours can all go to hell. Especially Mrs Carter in number three who leaves her bins out all week. If I did find a rock shaped like a frog, I would throw it at her.

## eBay

If I wanted a house full of cheap, dirty, second hand rubbish, I'd go to a garage sale in Klemzig.

## Email

People are always sending me all kinds of rubbish. Why would I want dozens of pictures of lots of love cats? I hate cats. I went away for a week recently and when I got back and checked my email, I had eight hundred and forty three emails. Eight hundred and forty of these were adverts for viagra and the other three were pictures of lots of love cats. I have a 'no junk mail' sticker on my computer but nobody has taken any notice.

## /b/

I spent a good hour on this site and still have no idea what it is for. All I could work out is that I am apparently a newfag and cannot triforce but am unsure as to why I would need to triforce in the first place. I asked some of the people on there for their advice regarding triforcing but the only answer I seemed to get was 'nigger'.

# Sad Caveman

# Hello, my name is Scott and I have a blog.

*As a professional blog writer of the wittiest stuff on the internet, I recently decided to quit my job as head assistant chef in charge of pickles at McDonalds and focus full time on my writing career. Due to my unique creative spark and rapier sharp wit, my blog has had unprecedented success and just this week I had another hit. Being a professional blog writer is not all Moët and chicken though, due to server and hosting fees, I made minus four hundred and ninety dollars last financial year but my wife works three jobs and has a credit card so it all balances out.*

If I had friends, they would often ask me, "Scott, what is the secret to writing a successful blog?" and I would explain to them that it is a gift and that some people are naturally born with an incredible creative spark while others just get to read it. Recently, I wrote about the time a bee flew in my car window and then flew back out. It was so funny and when I posted a link to it on a World of Warcraft forum, a level 54 mage wrote, "awesome man" which made my day. Once when I was online in my dwarf clan, I met a level 16 dwarf named Cindy and we fell in love despite her being below my status. I would send her poetry about Warcraft and she would edit it for me. As my wife works a hundred and eighty hour week, this gave me plenty of opportunity to organise a liaison with Cindy in real life.

Cindy turned out to be an actual dwarf. And a man. We still made love but I left feeling deceived and only partly satisfied. Why can't people just be honest?

Writing professionally is not my only creative outlet, I'm also a professional cartoonist. I am a much better drawer than Carl Schultz and my ideas are more clever and creative. Below is one of my best cartoons. When I originally posted it my hits went up 400% and all four people said that it was unlike any professional material they had ever seen before.

The cartoon above is funny on two levels, which makes it lateral. Firstly, I was looking at porn but said that I wasn't so this is like British comedy and brilliant in itself without the rest. Secondly, I said "make it so" which is what Captain Picard says in *Star Trek* and I was wearing my *Star Trek* uniform when I said it. Do you get it? It is probably too clever for you.

# Missing Missy

*I'm not a big fan of cats. If I visit your house, I do not want to pat your cat, sit on the couch where it has been, or have you make me a sandwich after patting it. I didn't want that sandwich anyway. The Maxwell House coffee was bad enough and when you smelled the milk to see if it was still okay, despite being a week past its use by date, I saw your nose touch the carton.*

*I actually rescued a cat once. I was walking across a bridge, over a river that was in flood, when I heard mewing and saw a frantic cat being pulled along. I picked up a fairly hefty branch and threw it over the rail to where the cat was. I did not see it after that but I am pretty sure it would have climbed on and ridden the branch to safety.*

**From:** Shannon Walkley
**Date:** Monday 21 June 2010 9.15am
**To:** David Thorne
**Subject:** Poster

Hi.

I opened the screen door yesterday and my cat got out and has been missing since then so I was wondering if you are not to busy you could make a poster for me.

It has to be A4 and I will photocopy it and put it around my suburb this afternoon.

This is the only photo of her I have she answers to the name Missy and is black and white and about 8 months old. missing on Harper street and my phone number.

Thanks Shan

**From:** David Thorne
**Date:** Monday 21 June 2010 9.26am
**To:** Shannon Walkley
**Subject:** Re: Poster

Dear Shannon,

That is shocking news. Luckily I was sitting down when I read your email and not half way up a ladder or tree. How are you holding up? I am surprised you managed to attend work at all what with thinking about Missy out there cold, frightened and alone... possibly lying on the side of the road, her back legs squashed by a vehicle, calling out "Shannon, where are you?"

Although I have two clients expecting completed work this afternoon, I will, of course, drop everything and do whatever it takes to facilitate the speedy return of Missy.

Regards, David

.....................................................................................

**From:** Shannon Walkley
**Date:** Monday 21 June 2010 9.37am
**To:** David Thorne
**Subject:** Re: Re: Poster

yeah ok thanks. I know you dont like cats but I am really worried about mine. I have to leave at 1pm today.

From: David Thorne
Date: Monday 21 June 2010 10.17am
To: Shannon Walkley
Subject: Re: Re: Re: Poster

Dear Shannon,

I never said I don't like cats. Once, having been invited to a party, I went clothes shopping beforehand and bought a pair of expensive G-Star boots. They were two sizes too small but I wanted them so badly I figured I could just wear them without socks and cut my toenails very short. As the party was only a few blocks from my place, I decided to walk.

After the first block, I lost all feeling in my feet. Arriving at the party, I stumbled into a guy named Steven, spilling Malibu & coke onto his white Wham 'Choose Life' t-shirt, and he punched me.

An hour or so after the incident, Steven sat down in a chair already occupied by a cat. The surprised cat clawed and snarled causing Steven to leap out of the chair, trip on a rug and strike his forehead onto the corner of a speaker; resulting in a two inch open gash.

In its shock, the cat also defecated, leaving Steven with a wet brown stain down the back of his beige cargo pants.

I liked that cat.

Attached poster as requested.

Regards, David

# MISSING MISSY

**A SHANNON PRODUCTION**

**From:** Shannon Walkley
**Date:** Monday 21 June 2010 10.24am
**To:** David Thorne
**Subject:** Re: Re: Re: Re: Poster

yeah thats not what I was looking for at all. it looks like a movie and how come the photo of Missy is so small?

...................................................................................

**From:** David Thorne
**Date:** Monday 21 June 2010 10.28am
**To:** Shannon Walkley
**Subject:** Re: Re: Re: Re: Re: Poster

Dear Shannon,

It's a design thing. The cat is lost in the negative space.

Regards, David.

...................................................................................

**From:** Shannon Walkley
**Date:** Monday 21 June 2010 10.33am
**To:** David Thorne
**Subject:** Re: Re: Re: Re: Re: Re: Poster

Thats just stupid. Can you do it properly please? I am extremely emotional over this and was up all night in tears. you seem to think it is funny. Can you make the photo bigger and fix the text please.

**From:** David Thorne
**Date:** Monday 21 June 2010 10.46am
**To:** Shannon Walkley
**Subject:** Re: Re: Re: Re: Re: Re: Re: Poster

Dear Shannon,

Having worked with designers for a few years now, I'd have assumed you understood, despite our vague suggestions otherwise, we do not welcome constructive criticism.

I don't come downstairs and tell you how to send text messages, log onto Facebook and look out of the window.

I will overlook this however, as you are no doubt preoccupied with thoughts of Missy attempting to make her way home across busy intersections or being trapped in a drain as it slowly fills with water. I spent three days down a well once but that was just for fun.

Amended poster as per your instructions.

Regards, David.

**From:** Shannon Walkley
**Date:** Monday 21 June 2010 10.59am
**To:** David Thorne
**Subject:** Re: Re: Re: Re: Re: Re: Re: Re: Poster

This is worse than the other one. can you make it so it shows the whole photo of Missy and delete the stupid text that says missing missy off it? I just want it to say lost.

**From:** David Thorne
**Date:** Monday 21 June 2010 11.14am
**To:** Shannon Walkley
**Subject:** Re: Re: Re: Re: Re: Re: Re: Re: Re: Poster

**From:** Shannon Walkley
**Date:** Monday 21 June 2010 11.21am
**To:** David Thorne
**Subject:** Re: Re: Re: Re: Re: Re: Re: Re: Re: Re: Poster

yeah can you do the poster or not? I just want a photo and the word lost and the telephone number and when and where she was lost and her name. Not like a movie poster or anything stupid. I have to leave early today. If it was your cat I would help you. Thanks.

...............................................................................................................

**From:** David Thorne
**Date:** Monday 21 June 2010 11.32am
**To:** Shannon Walkley
**Subject:** Awww

Dear Shannon,

I don't have a cat. I once agreed to look after a friend's cat for a week but after he dropped it off at my apartment and explained the concept of kitty litter, I kept the cat in a closed cardboard box in the shed and forgot about it. If I wanted to feed something and clean faeces, I wouldn't have put my mother in that home after her stroke. A week later, when my friend came to collect his cat, I pretended that I was not home and mailed the box to him. Apparently I failed to put enough stamps on the package and he had to collect it from the post office and pay eighteen dollars. He still goes on about that sometimes, people need to learn to let go. I have attached the amended version of your poster as per your detailed instructions.

Regards, David.

# LOST

## MISSY THE CAT

**MISSING FROM HARPER STREET
ON THE 20TH OF JUNE**

## CONTACT 0433 359 705

**From:** Shannon Walkley
**Date:** Monday 21 June 2010 11.47am
**To:** David Thorne
**Subject:** Re: Awww

Where did you get that photo from? Thats not my cat.

**From:** David Thorne
**Date:** Monday 21 June 2010 11.58am
**To:** Shannon Walkley
**Subject:** Re: Re: Awww

I know, but that one is cute. As Missy has probably met any one of several violent ends, it's possible you might get a better cat out of this. If anybody calls and says, "I haven't seen your orange cat but I did find a black and white one with its hind legs run over by a car, do you want it?" you can politely decline and save yourself a costly veterinarian bill.

I knew someone who had a basset hound that had its hind legs removed after an accident and it had to walk around with one of those little buggies with wheels. If it had been my dog, I would have asked for all its legs to be replaced with wheels and had a remote control installed. I'd charge neighbourhood kids for rides and enter it in races. If I did the same with a horse, I could drive it to work. I'd call it Steven.

Regards, David.

**From:** Shannon Walkley
**Date:** Monday 21 June 2010 12.07pm
**To:** David Thorne
**Subject:** Re: Re: Re: Awww

Please just use the photo I gave you.

**From:** Shannon Walkley
**Date:** Monday 21 June 2010 12.34pm
**To:** David Thorne
**Subject:** Re: Re: Re: Re: Re: Awww

I didnt say there was a reward. I dont have $2000 dollars.

What did you even put that there for? Apart from that it is perfect can you please remove the reward bit.

Thanks Shan.

# LOST

## MISSY THE CAT
## NO REWARD
### MISSING FROM HARPER STREET
### ON THE 20TH OF JUNE
## CONTACT 0433 359 705

**From:** Shannon Walkley
**Date:** Monday 21 June 2010 12.51pm
**To:** David Thorne
**Subject:** Re: Re: Re: Re: Re: Re: Re: Awww

Can you just please take the reward bit off altogether? I have to leave in ten minutes and I still have to make photocopies of it.

From: David Thorne
Date: Monday 21 June 2010 12.56pm
To: Shannon Walkley
Subject: Re: Re: Re: Re: Re: Re: Re: Re: Awww

LOST

MISSY THE CAT
MISSING FROM HARPER STREET
ON THE 20TH OF JUNE
CONTACT 0433 359 705

**From:** Shannon Walkley
**Date:** Monday 21 June 2010 1.03pm
**To:** David Thorne
**Subject:** Re: Re: Re: Re: Re: Re: Re: Re: Re: Awww

Fine. That will have to do.

# I Wish I Had a Monkey

*Not like the one in the above picture though, as it's kind of ugly and has some kind of fruit smeared all over its face. I'd want a clean monkey. Obviously having your own monkey would be fantastic for a host of reasons. Below is a list of the kind of monkeys that would be good to have. The list is far from complete as it omits Jetski Monkey, Boiling Water Monkey, and Battlestar Galactica Monkey, but covers the basic best kinds of monkeys.*

### Disguised Monkey

If I had a monkey, I would borrow a sewing machine and make my monkey a little monkey suit. Then if anyone said, "That's not a real monkey, it's just a monkey suit, I can see the zipper", I could say "I bet you fifty dollars it is a real monkey" and when they said "that seems like a reasonable bet", my monkey would take off the monkey suit and they would have to pay me fifty dollars. I would buy drugs with the fifty dollars. For the monkey. So he wouldn't mind spending his life in a monkey suit.

### Gambling Monkey

If I had a monkey, I would teach him to count cards like Dustin Hoffman in the movie *Rainman* and sneak my monkey into a casino. If anyone said, "Hey a monkey, whose monkey is that?" I would say, "It's not my monkey."

### Hairdressing Monkey

If I had a monkey, I would teach him how to do my hair - using the appropriate amount of product. I would then set the alarm for him to get up half an hour before I do and do my hair while I am still asleep. This would either give me more time in the morning or allow me to spend more time sleeping. I would just waste the extra half hour anyway so probably better to sleep but as I usually don't rock up to work till ten thirty or so, I could try leaving earlier. This would give me more time to write about what I would do if I had a monkey.

### Singing Monkey

If I had a monkey, I would teach it to sing Kylie Minogue songs. Then if Kylie passed out on stage again I would be able to save the day by having my monkey finish the concert for her. The concert promoters would probably give me free tickets and promotional gifts. Kylie would be so thankful that she might send me an autographed photo and I could sell it on eBay for fifty dollars. I would buy drugs with the fifty dollars. Not for the monkey, for me.

### Web Monkey

If I had a monkey, I would teach it to download porn for me. This way I could spend my time watching it instead of looking for it. I estimate this would save me one hundred and thirty hours a week. I would obviously require a monkey with similar tastes to mine but how hard can it be to find a monkey with a penchant for pregnant german women in latex?

## Paddling Monkey

If I had a monkey, I would teach it how to use a paddle. The next time I went kayaking I would be able to relax and enjoy the scenery while my monkey navigated the river. Also, the last time I went kayaking I was listening to my iPod and I fell asleep and got sunburnt and the current took me way up the river before I awoke when the kayak hit a tree branch and I had to paddle all the way back. Having a paddling monkey would prevent this ever happening again so really it's a safety thing.

## Channel Changing Monkey

If I had a monkey, I would teach it how to use all the entertainment equipment. I would save money on batteries for the remote controls by having my monkey change channels for me. With the money I saved on batteries, I would buy drugs. I would share the drugs with the monkey while we watched *Black Books* and Stephen Chow movies together.

## Surveillance Monkey

If I had a monkey, I'd teach it to track down people who annoy me on Facebook. Using earpieces to communicate, I would have my monkey conceal himself behind the person typing and when that person wrote something stupid, I would have my monkey run up and slap them on the back of the head really hard, then make a quick escape. Having several monkeys would be more convenient but I don't have time to train seven monkeys, what with having to do my own hair in the mornings.

## 5 Fun Things to do with a Monkey

Constructing and flying box kites. Eyetoy. Running down sand dunes. Playing Connect 4. Dressups.

## Yellow Shirt Monkey

If I had a monkey, I would name it Brendon. I would shave the monkey and buy a yellow shirt for it and teach it to write inane posts on Facebook. Occasionally I would burn the monkey with a cigarette lighter but not to cause enough damage to detract it from it's primary goal of impersonating a retard.

## Ceramic Monkey

If I had a monkey, I would name it Steve Darls and use it for scientific research. I would then publish my findings in a journal titled *Monkey Vs Electricity*. With the proceeds from the sale of this publication, I would buy a potters wheel and kiln, and produce my own range of contemporary statues of monkeys. I could make a cast of my dead monkey and use it to produce to-scale ceramic monkeys. I would design a sticker stating that part proceeds go to Greenpeace but would keep all the money for myself. With the money, I would buy drugs and spend my days stoned, turning pots.

# Flash Drive

*I do not get on all that well with my son's teacher. Since the day she gave him a brochure explaining 'the real meaning of Easter', I've had my eye on her. Recently, my offspring took a game called Tower Defense to school on his USB drive. As far as games are concerned, it's strategic and positive. At least it's not about stealing autos and shooting hookers. While I understand it was a breach of the rules, I do not feel being banned from using school computers is an appropriate punishment. I do however feel an appropriate punishment for handing out medieval metaphysic propaganda to children would be a good old-fashioned stoning.*

**From**: Margaret Bennett
**Date**: Friday 22 August 2009 3.40pm
**To**: David Thorne
**Subject**: computer room

Hello David

I tried to call you but your phone is off.

Just letting you know that Seb bought a flash drive to school yesterday and copied a game onto the school computers, which is against school rules, and he has been banned from using the computer room for the rest of the term.

Sincerely, Margaret

..............................................................................................

From: David Thorne
Date: Monday 24 August 2009 9.16am
To: Margaret Bennett
Subject: Re: computer room

Dear Maggie,

Thank you for your email. I am not answering my mobile phone at the moment due to a few issues with my landlord and neighbours. I am also experiencing iPhone envy and every second spent using my Nokia is like being trapped in a loveless marriage. Where you stay together for the kids. And the kids all have iPhones.

I was not aware that my son taking software to school was in breach of school rules. Although the game is strategic and public domain, not to mention that it was I who copied and gave it to him, I agree that banning him from access to the computers at school is an appropriate punishment. Especially considering his enthusiasm for the subject.

Also, though physical discipline is not longer administered in the public school system, it would probably be appropriate in this instance if nobody is watching. I know from experience that he can take a punch.

Regards, David

**From**: Margaret Bennett
**Date**: Tuesday 25 August 2009 10.37am
**To**: David Thorne
**Subject**: Re: Re: computer room

David

I would never strike a student and whether the software is pirated or not is not the issue. He denied having the drive which means he knew he shouldn't have it here then it was found in his bag so I feel the punishment is suitable.

Margaret

........................................................................................................

**From**: David Thorne
**Date**: Tuesday 25 August 2009 11.04am
**To**: Margaret Bennett
**Subject**: Re: Re: Re: computer room

Dear Maggie,

Yes, I agree. Education and access to the tools necessary for such should always come secondary to discipline.

When I was young, discipline was an accepted part of each school day. Once, when I coloured outside the lines, I was forced to stand in the playground with a sign around my neck that read 'non-conformist' while the other children pelted me with rubble from the recently torched school library. Apparently a copy of Biggles had been found behind a filing cabinet.

Another time, because I desperately wanted a Battlestar Galactica jacket like Apollo in the television series, using brown house paint from the shed at home, I painted my denim jacket and used Araldite to attach brass door hinges as clasps. Feeling that it was an excellent representation and despite the oil based paint still being wet, I wore it to school the next day. Unfortunately, the paint dried while I was sitting in Mrs Bowman's English class, securing me to the chair. After the school handyman cut me free, I was sent to the principal for damaging school property. My punishment was to scrape wads of chewing gum off the bottom of every chair in the school after hours. It took several weeks and it was during this lonely time that I created my imaginary friend Mr Wrigley. During class, when the teacher was not looking, we would pass each other notes regarding the merits of disciplinary action and how one day we would own real Battlestar Galactica jackets.

Also, if you happen to see Seb eating anything over the next few weeks, please remove the food from him immediately. He forgot to feed his turtle last week and I feel a month without food will help him understand both the importance of being a responsible pet owner and the effects of malnutrition.

Regards, David

..................................................................................................

**From**: Margaret Bennett
**Date**: Tuesday 25 August 2009 4.10pm
**To**: David Thorne
**Subject**: Re: Re: Re: Re: computer room

I assume you're not being serious about the food but I am forwarding your email to the principal as per school policy.

Dear Maggie,

Rest assured, I would not really withhold nutritional requirements from any child. I recently read somewhere that a healthy breakfast helps concentration and have found, since replacing my usual diet of nicotine with froot loops, I am able to move small objects with my mind.

Just this morning Seb and I were discussing the importance of good nutrition which is why, if you check in his school bag, you will find a bag of rice, vegetables, a wok and a camp stove. The gas bottle can be a little tricky but has instructions printed on the side so he should be alright. Please remind him to stand well back and cover his face while igniting as the hose is worn and has developed a small leak.

Also, I am not sure what you are teaching in your classroom but Seb came home last week talking about a healthy eating pyramid. I had to explain to him that pyramids are made of stone and therefore not edible so I would appreciate you not filling his head with these fanciful notions.

Regards, David

**From**: Margaret Bennett
**Date**: Wednesday 26 August 2009 2.05pm
**To**: David Thorne
**Subject**: Re: Re: Re: Re: Re: Re: computer room

I will speak to the principal about the ban but you have to understand that only government approved software is allowed on the computers and Seb knew this rule.

Margaret

....................................................................................................

**From**: David Thorne
**Date**: Wednesday 26 August 2009 2.17pm
**To**: Margaret Bennett
**Subject**: Re: Re: Re: Re: Re: Re: Re: computer room

Dear Maggie,

I understand the need for conformity. Without a concise set of rules to follow we would probably all have to resort to common sense. Discipline is the key to conformity and it is important that we learn not to question authority at an early age.

Just this week I found a Sue Townsend novel in Seb's bag that I do not believe is on the school approved reading list. Do not concern yourself about it making its way to the schoolyard however, as we attended a community book burning last night. Although one lady tried to ruin the atmosphere with comments regarding Mayan codices and the Alexandrian Libraries, I mentioned to the High Magus that I'd overheard her discussing spells to turn the village cow's milk sour, and the mob took care of the rest.

Regards, David

**From:** Margaret Bennett
**Date:** Thursday 28 August 2009 11.56am
**To:** David Thorne
**Subject:** Re: Re: Re: Re: Re: Re: Re: Re: computer room

I've spoken to the principal and in this instance we will lift the ban.

Margaret

# Breakthrough Medical Operation Brings New Hope For Thomas

*It was champagne all round last night in celebration of the medical breakthrough which, despite previous diagnostics, may indeed cure Thomas of the rare condition which has caused his head to swell to unimagined proportions.*

Dr Hermine Bergmann is thrilled with the results. "We have been able to reduce the swelling by 85%, bringing his head down to the size of a small family car or large hatchback, similar to the Renault my husband recently bought me," she said. "We have him wearing a two person inflatable boat as a hat to avoid any further damage, but we hope to have his head down to a size where he will be able to drive his convertible with the roof up."

Thomas' family are extremely pleased at the breakthrough, "I thought his head was just going to get bigger and bigger till it exploded," said his father, "He'd come over and sit down in front of the telly and nobody could see a thing past his great hairy weather balloon of a head. It was fucking incredible, you should have seen it. I would have taken photos but I didn't have a wide angle lens."

"The operation was touch and go there for a while" said Dr Bergmann, "We simply did not have medical instruments designed to cut through that amount of mass, even the industrial laser bought in especially for the operation struggled to get through the eighteen metres of solid limestone, but the patient is doing well and looking forward to one day being able to wear his trucker hats again."

Physicists have expressed relief at the news as it was widely considered that Thomas' head, if allowed to expand further, would develop its own gravitational field affecting planetary rotation.

*Thomas in his car.*

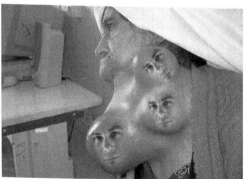

*Thomas' head badly Photoshopped onto a lady with goiters.*

# Kaleth the Adelaide Gothic

*Hello, my name is Kaleth. My real name is Darryl but my friends call me Kaleth. I asked them to and some of them said they would. I am a vampire and a creature of the night which is why my best friend Zothecula and I stand in the middle of the mall during the day discussing bats and being misunderstood.*

My cousin Justin wants to be a gothic but you can't just become a gothic - you are either creative and sensitive like I am or you're not. I agreed to meet him at the mall to stand in the middle and discuss bats and being misunderstood but when he got there it was obvious that his shirt was dark blue and not black so I hid. Yesterday, while Zothecula and I were standing in the middle of the mall discussing bats and being misunderstood, a group of people called me an Emu. I looked it up on Google and it turns out that it is a bird that can't fly so they were wrong because I can fly. Once, when I was a bat, I flew to my friend Zothecula's house and tapped on his window. The next day he told me that he saw a bat outside his window and I told him that it was me but he didn't believe me. I'm going to live forever because I'm a vampire.

Yesterday, while I was doing some gothic dancing, my neighbour banged on the wall. If he knew I could cast a magic spell that would kill him, he'd be a lot more careful.

Here are some of my paintings. I do them to show others the pain and torment I experience:

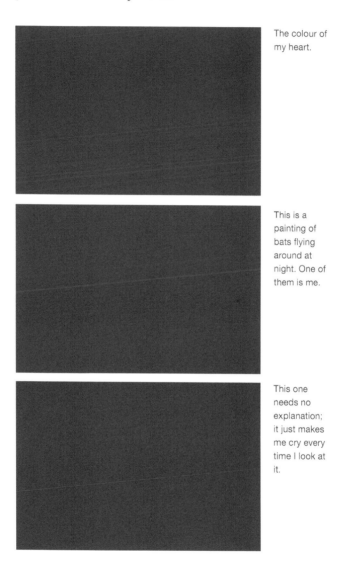

The colour of my heart.

This is a painting of bats flying around at night. One of them is me.

This one needs no explanation; it just makes me cry every time I look at it.

# Simon's Guide to Wilderness Survival

*Hello, my name is Simon and I have been lost thirty six times which makes me an expert. Once when I was lost in the desert, I survived by absorbing the moisture from the air through my skin like a frog.*

### Survival Tip #1 - Water

The trick to finding water in the wilderness is to remember that it always flows downhill. Find an incline and wait at the bottom.

### Survival Tip #2 - Food

Do not eat the bright purple mushrooms. I tried them once and discussed the differences between the director's cut of Bladerunner and the cinematic release with a beetle.

### Survival Tip #3 - Shelter

Building a shelter is an integral component of survival. A small bungalow or cottage will be sufficient unless you have a lot of furniture. Always remember that when tiling a roof, it's important to use a rope and harness to avoid falling. If you do fall, land horizontally with your arms and legs stretched out to maximise surface area. Always check with your local council on required permits prior to building.

Materials that are not suitable for building shelter with include water, angry words, and live ants.

### Survival Tip #4 - Fire

Forest fires are caused by lightning strikes so run a steel cable from the top of a tall tree to a pile of sticks and be patient.

### Survival Tip #5 - Clothing

If you are camping in a cool climate, such as the Antarctic, make sure to take a scarf.

### Survival Tip #6 - Rescue

If you are lost in a desert, writing a large SOS in the sand with your water is an effective means of drawing attention. If you are lost in a jungle, a simple two-way radio can be constructed from kits available at any Tandy or RadioShack store.

Waving your arms at passing rescue planes expends precious energy so it is better to dig a small hole, lay in it, cover yourself with leaves to keep warm and relax while you wait for them to find you. Use the time you are waiting to be rescued wisely. Sort your DVD collection by alphabetical order or fix that dripping tap you've been meaning to get to.

**MASSANUTTEN**
PROPERTY OWNERS ASSOCIATION

3980 MASSANUTTEN DRIVE MASSANUTTEN, VIRGINIA 22840 TEL: 540/289-9466 FAX: 540/289-9406
WEBSITE: www.massanuttenvillage.com EMAIL: mpoa@massanuttenvillage.com

Date: OCTOBER 6, 2010

To: Resident

Property: ~~████████~~e, Massanutten Village, VA, 22840

Offence: MPOA Section 9    No. 008731

**section 9 of the Massanutten Resident Agreement**

**9.** No trash may be put out before Sunday evening. Any trash not in a secured trash container or trash dispersed by animals may be picked up by MPOA employees and owner may be billed for cost. Bear proof trash cans have been provided at Hopkins Park and the MPOA pool located on Peak Drive for overflow or early check-out trash.

☐ **Trash placed for collection prior to Sunday evening**

☒ **Unsecured bags**

☐ **Unsecured Food Items**

- - - - - - - - - - - - - - - - - - - - - - - - - - - - - - - - - - - - - - - - - - - - - - - -

**Payments must made at the Property Owners Office located at 3980 Massanutten Drive during office hours Monday to Friday. Please bring property owner ID with you.**

Description of Offence:    Unsecured Trash

TOTAL AMOUNT DUE:    $75.00

NAME: _____

Payment by  ☐ Check  ☐ Card  ☐ Cash    Office Stamp:

112

# Massanutten

*Massanutten is a small four-seasons resort in Virginia, US, with a population currently comprising of two thousand old people, their cats, one Australian, his partner, and a dog named Further. Being an Australian, the town of Massanutten is like another planet to me. A heavily wooded planet founded by Norman Rockwell and colonised by John Deere tractor owners with a vision that included waterslides and mini-golf.*

*Along with mini-golf, waterslides, old people, cats, one Australian, his partner, and a dog named Further, Massanutten apparently has bears. I haven't seen any yet but that is only, I assume, due to most people following rules outlined in section 9 of the MPOA Agreement.*

**From:** David Thorne
**Date:** Thursday 7 October 2010 11.04am
**To:** mpoa@massanuttenvillage.com
**Subject:** Bears

Dear Sir and/or Madam,

I have received a request for seventy-five of my dollars for putting my trash out for collection without securing it inside a bear-proof container. Due to a series of events the night before, I forgot to put my trash out and had to run it out the next morning after hearing the collection truck approach.

As regulations govern only actions within certain defined limits and thereby justify all similar actions that lie outside those limits, I request that my offence is changed from 'unsecured trash' to 'secured trash barring the possibility of bears formulating a strategy in which to take advantage of the few minutes between deposit and collection.'

Regards, David

......................................................................................................

**From:** Patricia Jennings
**Date:** Thursday 7 October 2010 5.16pm
**To:** David Thorne
**Subject:** Re: Bears

Hello Mr. Thorne

Section 9 of the MPOA Agreement which you would have signed clearly states that trash must be secured. The reason we have these rules is so that bears and other large animals are not attracted to the area. This is for everyone's safety. All bear sightings should be reported immediately to the MPOA. A ladys cat was almost bitten by a bear just a few weeks ago near the mini golf course.

Patricia

**From:** David Thorne
**Date:** Thursday 7 October 2010 9.12pm
**To:** Patricia Jennings
**Subject:** Re: Re: Bears

Dear Pat,

Due to the abundant supply of cats in the area, I'm surprised bears bother with trash at all. As I have run over at least four cats this week and one of those did not put up much of a chase, it may be suggested that elderly residents and their cats pose more of an attraction for bears than unsecured trash. For the safety of all residents, section 9 of the MPOA Agreement should probably be amended to state that all cats, and their elderly owners, be kept in bear-proof containers.

While out walking this evening, I witnessed several cats having some kind of meeting on the sidewalk ahead of me. Possibly to discuss the local bear problem. After reading that a bear recently ate a ladies cat in the area and hearing a twig snap in the woods behind me, I took the shortest route home by cutting through the Massanutten mini-golf facilities. Managing to scale the three metre fence via fear and a trash can, I slipped, caught my back pants pocket on one of the pointy metal bars, and hung there for several minutes before managing to wriggle out of them - dropping to safety and to the right of hole 7. Fashioning temporary legwear by removing my jumper and placing my legs in the sleeves, figuring they would look like Hammer pants to people driving by, I left the premises by climbing the papier-mâché boulders near hole 16, leaping onto the ticket hut roof, and dropping down the other side to safety. If my shoes had not been wet and slippery from the pond to the right of hole 7, I am pretty sure I would have made it on the first attempt. While not pointing any blame, I quite liked those pants as they fit really well and cost around seventy-five dollars.

Also, as per your instructions to report bear sightings, I have attached a photograph taken outside my home a few minutes ago. I apologise for the quality but was fearful of getting too close as I've heard bears constrict and consume their prey whole, taking several days to fully digest. As I have a short attention span and would prefer a quick death, such as removing my helmet in space, I request you send assistance immediately.

Regards, David

From: Patricia Jennings
Date: Friday 8 October 2010 2.26pm
To: David Thorne
Subject: Re: Re: Re: Bears

I checked with Carol at the mini golf hut and no pants were found on the fence. I doubt any of that really happened. That's a dog with a blanket on it. I'm not going to waste anyone's time sending an officer out to check that.

**From:** David Thorne
**Date:** Friday 8 October 2010 2.51pm
**To:** Patricia Jennings
**Subject:** Re: Re: Re: Re: Bears

Dear Pat,

If Carol from the mini-golf hut has time to check the perimeter for pants, why not send her? While issuing me a seventy-five dollar fine by justifying it is for the safety of others, you seem pretty quick to dismiss mine. As people rely on your protection from bears and your position consists entirely of not waiving fines issued to ensure the compliance of regulations that protect people from bears, you should probably send out a memo or something stating that we are on our own in an emergency situation. On the back of the memo, you could include instructions on making a pointy stick to protect ourselves with.

I own a gun but am unsure if a bear, shot with a Daisy .177 calibre BB air rifle purchased from Wal-Mart for $39.75, would be wounded or just pissed off. While testing the rifle last week, my offspring was definitely the latter. I've heard the best way to protect yourself during a bear attack is to roll into a tight ball and cover your face but I am pretty sure a flame-thrower or a suit that metal spikes spring out of when you press a button would be more effective.

Although wary, after reading recently that a bear ate a lady and her cat in the area, I decided to risk leaving the premises in order to drive to your office and pay the fine. Unfortunately, possibly due to an unsecured Snickers bar on the dashboard, the bear is now in my vehicle and I am unable to do so. Please send assistance immediately as I have also run out of cigarettes and need to drive to the shop. If you send Carol, please ask her to stop on the way and grab me a pack.

While you may not class this as an emergency or possible danger to others, you haven't seen me after two hours without nicotine.

Regards, David

**From:** Patricia Jennings
**Date:** Friday 8 October 2010 3.18pm
**To:** David Thorne
**Subject:** Re: Re: Re: Re: Re: Bears

I won't be sending an officer because you're not in danger.. You have obviously just put a blanket on a dog while it is sitting in your car and taken a photo. If you want to express your opinion on trash collection rules you are welcome to attend the next MPOA community meeting which is held each month. Not understanding the importance of bear safety doesnt mean you dont have to follow the rules. I'm not even sure what your point is.

From: David Thorne
Date: Friday 8 October 2010 4.22pm
To: Patricia Jennings
Subject: Re: Re: Re: Re: Re: Re: Bears

Dear Pat,

My point is, barring the possibility of strategy formulating bears, stating my actions constitute a punishable breach of regulations structured to protect the community only enables you to be wrong with authority, not right.

Contrary to your statement, I do understand the importance of bear safety. Several years ago, I went camping with a few associates and thought it would be amusing to jump out of bushes while wearing a bear suit. Renting the only bear costume available, which was a koala, I altered it as best I could to make it look frightening by taping down the fluffy ears, adding sharp cardboard teeth and constructing two downward slanting eyebrows with electrical tape. While sitting around the campfire, I excused myself, donned the concealed costume and leapt out yelling 'Rawr'. Moments later, I realised the screaming and falling back off chairs wasn't due to me wearing a bear costume, but the fact I was standing in the fire while wearing a bear costume made of polyester.

After a two-hour drive to the nearest hospital, I underwent three weeks of skin grafting on my legs and several months hearing about how I ruined the camping trip. To this day, when anyone asks about the scars, I simply state, "It involved a camping trip and a bear, I don't like to talk about it," which is true; while I was in the hospital, my mother went to my apartment to get some clothes for me and found my porn collection so it's a touchy subject.

Also, while I was able to persuade the bear to exit my vehicle by pretending to be an old lady looking for her cat, it is now inside my premises. Although not immediately evident from the attached photograph, the bear is sitting between myself and the television remote control, located on the cushion to its left. As this effectively cuts off my ability to change channels and *The View* just started, this should be classed as an emergency situation. If I wanted to watch a group of old women carry on, I'd attend an MPOA community meeting.

Regards, David

**From:** Patricia Jennings
**Date:** Friday 8 October 2010 5.03pm
**To:** David Thorne
**Subject:** Re: Re: Re: Re: Re: Re: Re: Bears

I will waive the amount this time if you agree to make sure all your trash is secure in future.

**From:** David Thorne
**Date:** Friday 8 October 2010 5.16pm
**To:** Patricia Jennings
**Subject:** Re: Re: Re: Re: Re: Re: Re: Re: Bears

Dear Pat,

Regardless of whether you waive the fine or not, I will secure my trash. Not because it is a rule, but because it is a logical rule to follow.

Despite my continuing doubt as to the ability of bears to plan and execute manoeuvres requiring SWAT team precision, I will also secure my trash regardless of the time frame between deposit and collection. Not because it is a logical rule to follow, but because it is a rule.

How about you agree to waive the fine, and I promise not to email you the remaining eighty-six photos of my dog dressed as a bear.

Regards, David

...................................................................................................

**From:** Patricia Jennings
**Date:** Friday 8 October 2010 5.24pm
**To:** David Thorne
**Subject:** Re: Re: Re: Re: Re: Re: Re: Re: Re: Bears

Agreed.

# Hello, my name is Craig and I love dolphins.

*If I were a dolphin, I would be one of those brave ones that fights sharks. I'd swim alongside boats and jump out of the water to the awe of spectators and they would feed me fish. That would be heaps easier than catching them.*

I have devoted my life to collecting the most beautiful dolphin sculptures in the world. Here are just a few of my favourites:

As if mirroring the ocean, the waves sparkle with prismatic colors and dazzling lights. I have this on the dashboard of my car. At almost thirty inches it obstructs some view but is semi transparent so I do not feel it causes any problem.

The only way you'd sleep through this alarm is if you do it on porpoise. I love waking to the sound of dolphin calls, it makes me chipper, ready for the day, and aroused.

With a charmingly crafted shell for keepsakes, this decorative delight is a dolphin lover's dream! I keep this on my desk at work and use the hanging basket to put my mobile phone in. My ringtone is a dolphin call so whenever someone calls me, it's like the dolphin is singing.

Seashell, dolphins, and coral reef night light. Simply beautiful. If I was a dolphin, I would definitely live in an underwater paradise like this. Leith and I would be the dolphins on the right and the other dolphin would be a friend dropping by. They would remark on what a beautiful home we had and then we would eat that fish.

One of my favourites, three marbelized dolphins form a cosy nest, awaiting the pleasant aromas which will soon drift from the urn of this absolutely stunning oil warmer. Sometimes I light a candle, add my favourite oil, and sit watching it while listening to dolphin calls on my iPod.

A mother dolphin teaches her baby the ways of the sea on this blue-glass carved art piece If I was the mother dolphin, I would teach my baby dolphin that life has no set path but that which we choose.

# Statements My Offspring Has Made

*Sometimes I can't work out my offspring Seb. One moment he will state something that catches me off guard with its clarity, and then say something that causes me to think there may have been a mix-up in the hospital. I was called into his school to speak with the teacher recently. Her statement, "He has a good sense of humour but he's the only one that gets it," slightly concerned me, but her explanation of why he had received three detentions made me laugh, which was probably not the expected reaction:*

*Detention 1: Raised his hand during maths class and asked, "If Kate (a large girl in his class) did not eat for five weeks, would she get skinny or die?"*

*Detention 2: After teachers had calmed down a very upset child, it was discovered that Seb had told her, "I heard the teachers saying that your parents died today and you are going to have to live at the school."*

*Detention 3: While the principal was explaining the 'no nut policy' during a school assembly, Seb yelled out, "Thats a lot of nuts" after watching the movie Kung Pow the night before.*

### Money

"If I had a million dollars I would buy a house with big robot legs."

### Paying $7.50 for a coffee

"We should open up a shop next to that one, buy their coffees and sell them from our shop for a dollar more."

### Our four-door Mazda sedan

"We should paint flames on the side. Girls like cars with flames on the side. You will never get a girlfriend in a car that looks like this."

### DVD rental prices

"It makes no sense, this one is four dollars for a whole week and this one is six dollars for one night. It is backwards. Someone should tell them."

### After being offered a yoghurt sample in a supermarket

"She was nice, you should ask her to be your girlfriend before someone else does."

### Paying for petrol

"Leaves burn, why can't we just fill our car up with them? They are free."

### On being asked in an elevator what he wants to be when he grows up

"Either a model or a police sniper."

### Girls

"You can't trust girls. When I get a girlfriend, I'm not going to tell her where I live or work."

### On his minibike being stolen

"I hope they are riding it and the petrol tank blows up and their legs and arms get blown off and when they are in the hospital they think, 'I really wish I hadn't stolen that motorbike'."

### The supermarket

"If they made the aisles wider we could drive our car in and grab things through the window and pay on the way out like at McDonalds."

### Explaining Grand Theft Auto to his grandmother

"I don't shoot everybody, just the drug dealers and hookers."

### 2001 A Space Odyssey

"This movie is so boring. I would rather be staring at the wall and holding my breath for two hours."

### Static electricity

"If I am standing on carpet and I get electrocuted, does everybody in the room die apart from me?"

### Being told that the park belongs to everybody

"We should buy a fence and make people pay us two dollars to get in."

### Swimming

"If you swim in the sea then you should always go swimming with a fat girl because sharks will go for her first."

### Shoplifting

"If we went into a shop and I put a stereo on and danced, you could run out with a different stereo while everyone is looking at me."

### Cleaning

"It will just get messy again. I like it like this, it shows we have better things to do than cleaning."

### Marriage

"If you get married, do you have to let your wife look at your penis?"

### Homosexuality

"That's gross. Not the bit about girls kissing girls though, that's pretty good."

### School

"I don't understand why I have to go to school at all, the Internet knows more than all the teachers there put together."

### Hygiene

"You should never wash your hands because then you will have more germs than everything else and germs won't go on you because there is no room."

### Personalized Plates

"We should get the words 'Bad Boys' on our number plate. That way when people are behind us at the traffic lights, they wont mess with us. If they do, we can just lock the doors."

### Furniture

"We should sell everything we own and use the money to buy something nice instead."

### Jack

"That seems like a good deal to me. I would much rather have magic beans than a cow."

### Messy room

"What's a brothel? Is it a kind of soup?"

### New Pants

"I've never even heard of Corduroy. I hope you kept the receipt."

# Hello, my name is Mark and I have head lice.

I still remember the day the school nurse declared, "Mark, you have head lice." I felt as though I had been chosen.

Having head lice can be a very rewarding experience. As their host, it is important to provide them with the necessities of life. Once a week, I give my hair a light spray with chicken stock. In summer I do this daily. At Easter, I add a small of amount of chocolate to the mixture and at Christmas, I make them small presents using tweezers and a magnifying glass.

I've found with great care, your head lice community will thrive and are even transferable to other parts of your body. I currently have my hair buddies, as I like to call them, living not only on my head, but also in my eyebrows, eyelashes and armpits. When I am at the movie theatre, I like to pick head lice out of my hair and place them onto the heads of people in front of me, thus helping my head lice colonise new territories.

I talk to my head lice and play them tunes on my acoustic guitar. Sometimes when it is very quiet and I concentrate, I can hear them talking to each other and once I'm pretty sure I heard my name mentioned.

# "Hello Sir, my name is Jason and I was wondering if your company would be interested in a good drawer? No? Thank you for your time."

People often say to me, "Jason, you are a good drawer," and I say, "Thank you." Each fortnight, eighteen dollars (twenty percent) of my income is spent on charcoal and butcher's paper. It's an investment in my future.

Here are some of my drawings. They are all for sale. Please contact me immediately if you wish to purchase any of these masterpieces because I'm living in my car.

**Title**
Whale Looking For Mate
**Media**
Charcoal on butcher paper
**Price**
$2,800

**Name**
Nina in Floral Dress, Summertime
**Media**
Charcoal on butcher paper
**Price**
$5,200

**Title**
Friendly Tiger
**Media**
Charcoal on butcher paper
**Price**
$3,000

**Title**
My MacBook Pro
**Media**
Charcoal on butcher paper
**Price**
$4,500

# Nigerian Email

*Local captain of most teams, including the Lucius fan club, is safe after his 'safari to riches' became a living nightmare.*

"Mr Bandabaloobi told me he was from the Nigerian Bank," said Lucius, "We first met when he wrote me an email explaining a rich old guy had died and the government was going to keep his money unless I wanted it."

"I gave them my account details and bought a plane ticket to Nigeria to meet Mr Bandabaloobi. Once I arrived, I was beaten and taken to a small hotel room where I was stripped and kissed by dark, hairy men. One of the men, Carl, was very gentle and he told me he loved me. The others were very rough. I struggled and told them I was a friend of Mr Bandabaloobi but they tied me up and took turns kissing my beautiful body - something I've imagined but never expected to happen because I'm straight. Having returned home, my only regret is that I missed my meeting with Mr Bandabaloobi and didn't get to see those African animals that peek up really quick and look around and then pop back down really quick. I can't remember what they're called but they're very similar to those little dogs that live on the prairie. I can't remember what those ones are called either but they look a little bit like otters. They don't live in water like otters though, they live on the prairies. No, I don't know what a prairie is."

# One Girl, Twelve Cups

*Due to there being an unprecedented twelve coffee cups needing to be cleaned in the sink at work this morning, it is understandable that Shannon would be outraged by this intrusion on her Facebook and looking out the window time. Though kitchen duties may be an expected part of her job role, there is no reason why everyone should not reschedule work/client commitments and help out to ensure Shannon's social networking and looking out the window time is not interrupted.*

**From:** Shannon
**Date:** Monday 17 August 2009 10.12am
**To:** Staff
**Subject:** Coffee cups

There were twelve coffee cups left in the sink this morning. Could you please wash coffee cups after using them.

Thanks, Shan

**From:** David Thorne
**Date:** Monday 17 August 2009 10.19am
**To:** Shannon
**Subject:** Re: Coffee cups

Morning Shannon,

My apologies. Those coffee cups were mine. I have a busy schedule today so decided to have all of my coffee breaks this morning rather than taking twelve separate breaks throughout the day.

I'm experiencing severe heart palpitations but am also typing at four hundred and seventy words per minute so should be able to leave early.

Regards, David

---

**From:** Shannon
**Date:** Monday 17 August 2009 10.31am
**To:** David Thorne
**Subject:** Re: Re: Coffee cups

I wasn't saying they were all your coffee cups.

I was just saying that I shouldnt have to wash twelve coffee cups when I don't drink coffee. People should wash their own coffee cups or at least take it in turns to wash them.

**From:** David Thorne
**Date:** Monday 17 August 2009 10.42am
**To:** Shannon
**Subject:** Re: Re: Re: Coffee cups

Shannon,

Perhaps you could construct some kind of chart.

A roster system would enable us to work in an environment free of dirty coffee cups and put an end to any confusion regarding who the dirty coffee cup responsibility lies with.

David

........................................................................................

**From:** Shannon
**Date:** Monday 17 August 2009 1.08pm
**To:** Staff
**Subject:** Kitchen Roster

Hi everyone.

I have discussed a kitchen roster with David and feel it would be fair if we took it in turns to do the dishes. I have put the roster in the kitchen so everyone can remember.

I'm Monday morning and Wednesday and Friday afternoon.

David is Monday afternoon and Wednesday morning.

Lillian is Tuesday morning and Thursday afternoon.

Thomas is Tuesday afternoon and Friday morning.

Thanks, Shan

**From:** David Thorne
**Date:** Monday 17 August 2009 1.22pm
**To:** Shannon
**Subject:** Colour coded coffee cup cleaning chart

Shannon,

I notice that you have colour coded the coffee cup cleaning chart. While I appreciate the creative effort that has gone into it, the light salmon colour you have chosen for my name is very effeminate. I'm sure you have not done this on purpose and are not inferring anything, but I would appreciate you rectifying this immediately.

Would it be possible to swap colours with Thomas as he has quite a nice dusty blue.

Thank you, David

.....................................................................................

**From:** Shannon
**Date:** Monday 17 August 2009 2.17pm
**To:** Staff
**Subject:** Updated kitchen roster

Hi.

I have changed David's colour to blue on the kitchen roster. Thomas is now green.

**From:** Thomas
**Date:** Monday 17 August 2009 2.24pm
**To:** David Thorne
**Subject:** What the fuck?

What the fuck is this email from Shannon? I'm not doing a fucking kitchen roster. Was this your idea?

.....................................................................................

**From:** David Thorne
**Date:** Monday 17 August 2009 2.38pm
**To:** Thomas Cc: Shannon
**Subject:** Re: What the fuck?

Thomas, do you feel it is fair that Shannon should have to wash everyone's coffee cups? Apparently this morning there were twelve coffee cups in the sink.

I was planning to schedule a staff board meeting this afternoon to discuss the issue but Shannon has prepared a colour coded coffee cup cleaning chart for us instead.

We should all thank Shannon for taking the initiative and creating a system that will empower us to efficiently schedule client meetings and work commitments around our designated coffee cup cleaning duties. If at any stage our rostered coffee cup cleaning commitments coincide with work requirements, we can simply hold the client meeting in the kitchen - we can wash while the clients dry.

Today it may only be twelve coffee cups but tomorrow it could be several plates and a spoon. Then where would we be?

David

**From:** Thomas
**Date:** Monday 17 August 2009 2.56pm
**To:** Shannon
**Subject:** Kitchen stuff

Shannon, I don't need a chart telling me when to wash dishes. I'm not going to stop in the middle of writing proposals to wash cups.

David is being a fuckwit. I only use one coffee cup and I always rinse it out after I use it. If we have clients here and they use coffee cups then it is appreciated that you wash them as part of your job.

Thomas

....................................................................................................

**From:** Lillian
**Date:** Monday 17 August 2009 3.06pm
**To:** Thomas
**Subject:** Re: Kitchen stuff

What's this kitchen roster thing?

Did you agree to this?

**From:** David Thorne
**Date:** Monday 17 August 2009 3.09pm
**To:** Shannon
**Subject:** Rescheduling coffee cup duties

Shannon, can I swap my rostered coffee cup cleaning duty this afternoon for Thursday?

I've been busy all day and not had time to familiarise myself with correct coffee cup cleaning requirements. I am happy to reschedule my meetings tomorrow to undertake a training session on dish washing detergent location and washcloth procedures with you if you have the time.

I also feel it would be quite helpful if, prior to the training session, you prepared some kind of Powerpoint presentation. Possibly with graphs.

Will I need to bring my own rubber gloves or will these be provided?

David

........................................................................................

**From:** Shannon
**Date:** Monday 17 August 2009 3.20pm
**To:** David Thorne
**Subject:** Re: Rescheduling coffee cup duties

Whatever.

# Hello, my name is John and I ride a bicycle.

*My bicycle has a titanium composite alloy such as NASA uses on the space shuttle and has Shimano gears, which are the best. People often say to me "That's a nice bicycle John" and I reply, "Yes, it's made out of a titanium composite alloy such as NASA uses on the space shuttle and has Shimano gears ,which are the best."*

Sometimes when I'm riding my bicycle, I feel like I'm the only person on the road. If I have my earphones in and my iPod turned up really loud, I can't hear the car horns and people yelling, "Get off the fucking road." Little compares to the exhilaration of listening to Queen's Bicycle while riding in the centre of a lane at half the speed limit with several hundred cars banked up behind me during peak hour traffic.

Correct bicycling speed and position:

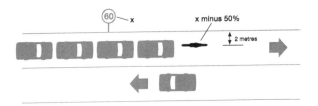

Riding a bicycle has many advantages. As you don't have to register it or obey road rules, I'm currently constructing a family bicycle consisting of two frames welded together with four armchairs in between. Due to the extra weight, I've added an engine and devised a roof, doors and storage area at the back to allow us to ride in all weather conditions and take it shopping.

Seat constructed by a team of physicists using the largest and most expensive laser on earth.

Titanium composite alloy frame such as NASA uses on the space shuttle.

Handle bars made from a Polycarbonate fibre from the future.

Brakes made from Pretanium, a metal not yet discovered by man.

Tyres made from rubber collected from a rare tree in the Amazon by tribal elders.

Shimano gears because they are the best.

Pedals formed by pressure in the lower atmosphere of Jupiter.

I'm often asked why my Spandex outfit features several hundred corporate sponsorship logos even though I do not actually have a sponsor. The reason for this is simple: For every thirty male bicycle riders there is one female bicycle rider and, as in nature where the most adorned peacock gets the peahen, the male bicycle rider with the most brightly coloured Spandex and most corporate sponsorship logos gets to mate with her.

Things that are almost as good as riding my bicycle:

1. Looking at my bicycle
2. Talking about my bicycle
3. Watching television programs about bicycles
4. Cheese

# Hello, my name is Lucius and I'd like you to sign here, please.

*I'm probably the best courier in the world. If you have a box and you want it to go somewhere, I will come and get it and take it there instead of you having to do it yourself. You have to pay me to do it but it saves you time so it is worth it. It doesn't matter what kind of box, once I delivered a box full of bolts which was really heavy. I'm very strong though. The customer said, "Wow, that box looks heavy." and I replied "No, it's light for me."*

## PICKUP & DELIVERY LOG

### 8.30am

The first pick up and delivery of the day is always the best. I try to guess what colour the box will be and what will be in it. If the tape on the box is the kind you can lift and put back, I have a look. Sometimes it's food. I don't eat it though as that would be against the Courier Code. Once, there was a whole box of sandwiches for a work function and they wouldn't have noticed if I'd eaten one but I didn't. I took a little bit out of each sandwich but that is allowed.

## 9.45am

YES! It was a brown box! I knew it would be a brown box. I have definitely got psychotic powers. I have guessed the box would be brown 840 times in a row, which proves my powers are probably the most powerful in the world. I have to keep my powers a secret though as the government would want to control someone as powerful as I probably am. I would have to live my life on the run, never settling down in one place for long. The government would probably hunt me down and fifty of them would point their guns at me and I would concentrate and the guns would float up in the air or turn into snakes and the men would say, "He is more powerful than we thought possible."

I pulled up around the corner to have a look inside the box but it was just books which was disappointing.

## 10.30am

I delivered the box and the girl in the front foyer signed and printed her name. Her name is Kate and I could tell she thought I was one of the top five best lookingest guys in Adelaide and wished I was her boyfriend. I told her about my psychotic powers and was going to ask her out but she was really busy and had to get back to work. I will see her again later today though as the company she works for is a regular client. I'll write her a poem in my lunch break.

On the way out the door I took a couple of photos of her on my camera phone. She looks a bit surprised in the first photo and blurry in the second as she was getting out of her chair as the door closed. I will use the flash next time. It is somewhere in settings. When anyone has a problem with their phone they always get me to fix it because I am like a computer genius. I'd probably be the biggest computer genius in the world but I can't be bothered learning all that stuff.

**11.15am**

Stuck in traffic on my way to the next box pickup. I feel it might be brown. I like to listen to music while I am waiting and have *Arrival*, *Super Trouper* and *Waterloo* recorded onto TDK Cassette. When I make the final payment on my delivery van in fourteen years, I'm going to have a CD Player installed. I saw them at Kmart for only $49.95 so I'm saving for one. When I'm waiting in traffic, I turn the music up as loud as it will go. Sometimes I become lost in the beat and imagine that I am Paula Abdul dancing with the cartoon cat on the stairs in that music clip where she dances with the cartoon cat on the stairs. I am also probably one of the best singers in the world and when my friend Jedd is in the van, I say to him, "Make me that beat already, so I can destroy it, with my unstoppable flows," and he does.

**12.45pm**

841! It's a big box too - priority pickup from one hospital to another. I should not have looked inside this one. I will deliver it after I finish my lunch break and sponge wash. I always keep a wet sponge in the back and when I park the van for lunch, I undress and sponge myself down so that I am clean and refreshed for the rest of the day.

I stopped off at Target and bought cologne and a suit, I am going to wear it for Kate. I have also written her a poem:

*Kate by Lucius*
I delivered you a box today.
It was brown with clear tape wrapped around it.
I'm in the back of my van looking at photos of you.
Imagining you opening the box.
I don't know what's in it because I didn't look.
The tape was like that when I picked it up.

144

### 3.20pm

I just left the hospital. They were quite rude. A nurse said that she was going to ring my boss and I told her, "He might be the boss of me but I am the boss of my life" which was obviously too philosophical for her because she just stood there looking at me. She was completely porned. If I were a transformer she would be so sorry. I took a whole bunch of latex gloves while she was not looking and am on my way to pick up a box to be delivered to the company that Kate works for.

I have a strong feeling that this box will be brown and I will drive really fast to get it to her quickly so she sees how professional and efficient I am. I am probably the best driver in the world and if I were a racing car driver, I would be world champion.

### 3.50pm

842! I had to climb six flights of stairs to collect the box but I am very fit and athletic as I own a trampoline and do four hours of air running every night. Air running is where you jump really high then run as fast as you can in the air. It's good for the vascular system and often my neighbours come out to watch me. If it was a team sport I would be captain.

I'm on my way to deliver the box to Kate. I can't wait to see her and I bet she is as excited as I am. I changed into my suit and put on the cologne. I will stand very close to her so that she can smell it. I have cleaned the van up a little bit as I will ask her to come for a ride.

Also, I read somewhere that girls like it when you ask them about themselves so in addition to the poem, I have compiled a list of questions for her to fill out about where she lives and what she does.

**5.10pm**

I'm on my way back to the depot as my boss rang and said he needs to see me immediately. Probably to give me a raise or promotion.

I delivered the box and Kate absolutely loved her poem, I read it out to her and she was speechless. There were tears in her eyes and she was shaking so I could tell she was overcome with emotion. She couldn't come for a ride in my van because she had a dentist appointment but I could tell she wanted to. She asked my full name and then repeated it to someone on the phone so I know she feels the same way I do if she is telling her friends about me. I will buy her lunch tomorrow and surprise her by taking it in and eating it there with her.

I will say, "Special delivery!" and when she asks what it is, I will reply, "Me. And a Subway footlong."

# Have you ever noticed the beauty of a baby's smile?

*Hello, my name is Barry. I was born in a small village near a secret government testing complex. As part of an experiment in human/pig cloning, I led a happy childhood, often seen rolling through the streets of the village. When I grew to manhood, I was placed inside a magnetically shielded device designed to compress my molecular structure into a singularity point using my body's own gravitational field. Now that I am a singularity point, I have the ability to see through all time and space.*

I'm available and looking for that special woman. She has to enjoy never leaving the house, cleaning me with a damp cloth and experiencing the beauty of a baby's smile. I placed an ad in the singles columns that simply read 'Woman wanted'. I felt it would be superficial to include that she must be athletic and named Candy, I will screen them when they call.

*The View From My Bed* A Poem by Barry
I have two buckets, green and blue.
On Tuesdays a nurse comes and cleans my poo.

*Light fitment broken.*

## STEVENSON
### STRATA MANAGEMENT

D34

| OWNER: Z. VULICG | INSPECTION DATE: 30.9.09 |
|---|---|
| TENANT: THORNE / DAVID | INSPECTION BY: Peter |
| PROPERTY ADDRESS: | |

| | G | A | P | COMMENTS/SUGGESTIONS |
|---|---|---|---|---|
| ENTRY HALL | | | | |
| PASSAGES | | | | |
| LOUNGE ROOM | | | | woodwork requires attention including front door |
| DINING ROOM | | | | |
| KITCHEN | | ✓ | | tiles grubby. Stove burners req cleaning |
| FAMILY ROOM | | | | |
| BEDROOM 1 | | ✓ | | |
| BEDROOM 2 | | ✓ | | |
| BEDROOM 3 | | | | |
| BEDROOM 4 | | | | |
| STUDY | | | | shower base grubby, |
| BATHROOM | | ✓ | | extractor fan filthy. |
| ENSUITE | | | | |
| TOILET 1 | | | | |
| TOILET 2 | | | | |
| LAUNDRY | | | | |
| GARAGE/CARPORT | | | | |
| SHED/W.SHOP | | | | |
| PATIO | | | | |
| POOL | | | | |
| FRONT GARDEN | | | | Side fence has been replaced |
| REAR GARDEN | | | | |
| WATER METER | | | | |
| | | | | |
| | | | | |

GENERAL COMMENTS

Property is not being maintained
to a satisfactory condition.
walls, paintwork, tiles all require cleaning.
Apartment smells of smoke; This is a
no smoking tenancy agreement

G - GOOD   A - AVERAGE   P - POOR

Property to be Re-Inspected
in two weeks time.

148

# Grubby Tenant

*Peter's profile on his company's website declares that Peter, an assistant rental manager, enjoys watching cricket, coin collecting, and once swam with sharks.*

*I'm not a great fan of rental property inspections but they are preferable to rental property inspections without warning. Especially if you are not home at the time and you haven't cleaned since the Columbus disaster. And you left an adult film on top of the television in the bedroom. Next to drugs. One of the worst adult films I have ever seen was called 'Debbie Does Dallas' which featured a lot of scenes with people wearing clothes and talking about things and, because the movie was shot in the seventies, looked like they were wearing shorts made out of hair when they finally did get naked.*

*The worst adult movie I have ever seen was titled 'Marge & Me Xmas 94' which I discovered inside a second hand Betamax video recorder I bought for thirty five dollars. While it contained a lot of nudity, most of it hairless, and very little dialogue apart from Marge complaining continuously about a cramp and at one point the gas bill, they were both overweight and well into their sixties so I could only handle an hour or so before ejecting the tape in disgust.*

**From:** David Thorne
**Date:** Wednesday 30 September 2009 6.04pm
**To:** Peter Williams
**Subject:** Inspection Report

Dear Peter,

Thank you for the surprise inspection and invitation to participate in the next. I appreciate you underlining the text at the bottom of the page which I would otherwise have surely mistaken for part of the natural pattern in the paper. I was going to clean the apartment but had so many things on my 'to do' list that I decided to treat them all equally and draw pictures of sharks instead. I have attached one for your honest appraisal.

Regards, David

.......................................................................................................

**From:** Peter Williams
**Date:** Thursday 01 October 2009 9.41am
**To:** David Thorne
**Subject:** Re: Inspection Report

David

I recommend you take this matter more seriously. You were sent notice of the inspection as part of our normal procedure. In addition to the cleaning, the light fitting in the lounge room is broken and the apartment smells of smoke.

Peter

**From:** David Thorne
**Date:** Thursday 01 October 2009 10.26am
**To:** Peter Williams
**Subject:** Re: Re: Inspection Report

Dear Peter,

The light fitting was the victim of a toy lightsaber being swung in a space too small to do the same with a cat. I dodged a leaping double handed overhead attack and the fitting, being fitted, didn't. I will grab a matching replacement $12 fitting from IKEA the next time I require a tiny ironing board or glass tea light.

The smell you mistook for cigarette smoke was probably just from my fog machine. Each Tuesday I hold a disco in my bedroom with strobe lighting and a special guest. As my wardrobe door has a large mirror on it, it looks like someone is dancing with me. I once dressed as a lady and it was almost exactly what I imagine dancing with a real lady would be like.

You should come one night; it will be a dance spectacular. I imagine you are probably a good dancer because you are small and the smallest member of the Rocksteady Crew was the best one.

Regards, David

**From:** Peter Williams
**Date:** Thursday 01 October 2009 1.16pm
**To:** David Thorne
**Subject:** Re: Re: Re: Inspection Report

I don't appreciate being called small or being sent drawings of me being eaten by a shark. The apartment is to be cleaned and reinspected in two weeks time. You can't use a fog machine in the apartment due to possible smoke damage.

Peter

........................................................................................

**From:** David Thorne
**Date:** Thursday 01 October 2009 4.02pm
**To:** Peter Williams
**Subject:** Re: Re: Re: Re: Inspection Report

Dear Peter,

I apologise for mentioning your smallness. Both the Rocksteady Crew comment and drawing were uncalled for. Especially as the unclear dimensions of the shark made it seem like you were the size of a small fish.

Please find attached a revised version.

Regards, David

**From:** Peter Williams
**Date:** Thursday 01 October 2009 5.12pm
**To:** David Thorne
**Subject:** Re: Re: Re: Re: Re: Inspection Report

David

Do not send me any more drawings. I keep a record of everything you send just so you know. If the apartment is not clean when we reinspect in two weeks time, we will consider terminating the lease as we have also had ongoing noise complaints regarding the premises.

Peter

..................................................................................................

**From:** David Thorne
**Date:** Thursday 01 October 2009 6.27pm
**To:** Peter Williams
**Subject:** Re: Re: Re: Re: Re: Re: Inspection Report

Dear Peter,

Yes, I find loud music helps me relax while I clean as the music distracts me so much that I stop cleaning. Which is relaxing.

I will get onto it this week though as I do not wish to be evicted. I have severe agoraphobia and residing in an apartment where I can reach all four walls while standing in the one spot brings me a feeling of security.

Also, the daily culling of plague proportion cockroaches gives me something to do in my spare time. I class the eighteen cans of surface spray I use per week as sporting equipment. I purchased one of those electronic things that plugs into the wall which is meant to scare cockroaches by sending a pulse through the apartment wiring but, while it has reduced the numbers, it seems others have evolved to feed off the electrical signal, increasing their size. I am using one as a coffee table in the lounge and two smaller ones as side tables in the bedroom.

Regards, David

..................................................................................

**From:** Peter Williams
**Date:** Friday 02 October 2009 10.18am
**To:** David Thorne
**Subject:** Re: Re: Re: Re: Re: Re: Re: Inspection Report

Clean the property or we will terminate the lease - the choice is yours. Don't email me again unless it is of a serious matter.

Peter

..................................................................................

**From:** David Thorne
**Date:** Friday 02 October 2009 10.36am
**To:** Peter Williams
**Subject:** Nom nom nom

# Chatroulette

*The problem with video based communication is that people can see you. As it takes me at least four hours just to do my hair, this is simply not practical. I generally write in tracksuit pants and t-shirt while eating pizza, which would be unfair to the other parties to have to view.*

*Regardless, having heard a lot about Chatroulette recently, I decided to have a look. For every ten video connections, eight of them were fat people playing with their penis. Apart from a couple of interesting people I met, it was possibly the most pointless website I have ever been on.*

Partner

You

☐ Auto start   ☑ Clean chatlog   ☐ Chat sounds

>Connected

hi

Hello. Star Wars fan?

no

What's the deal with the Chewbacca costume then?

> Your partner disconnected. Reconnecting...

---

Partner

You

☐ Auto start   ☑ Clean chatlog   ☐ Chat sounds

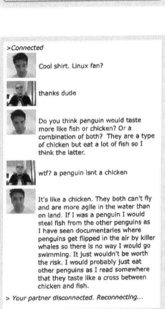

>Connected

Cool shirt. Linux fan?

thanks dude

Do you think penguin would taste more like fish or chicken? Or a combination of both? They are a type of chicken but eat a lot of fish so I think the latter.

wtf? a penguin isnt a chicken

It's like a chicken. They both can't fly and are more agile in the water than on land. If I was a penguin I would steal fish from the other penguins as I have seen documentaries where penguins get flipped in the air by killer whales so there is no way I would go swimming. It just wouldn't be worth the risk. I would probably just eat other penguins as I read somewhere that they taste like a cross between chicken and fish.

> Your partner disconnected. Reconnecting...

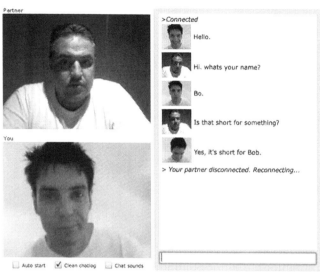

Partner

You

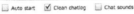

☐ Auto start   ☑ Clean chatlog   ☐ Chat sounds

>*Connected*

 hello how ar you?

 About time. I have been waiting for over twenty minutes. This is possibly the worst online support I have ever experienced. I purchased a stereo from you guys two weeks ago and the remote control did not come with batteries. Is this an omission or am I expected to purchase my own? I have the new Miley Cyrus CD and was looking forward to boot-scooting. Did you know that she is Billy Ray Cyrus's daughter? That is simply way too much talent to be in one family. What's your favourite Billy Ray Cyrus song?

> *Your partner disconnected. Reconnecting...*

---

Partner

You

☐ Auto start   ☑ Clean chatlog   ☐ Chat sounds

>*Connected*

 Hello my name is mike i am in germany i am a student and am 24 old. How are you today and where are you today what country are you in. are you well?

 Whoa there Charles Dickens. I didn't sign on here to proof read a novel.

> *Your partner disconnected. Reconnecting...*

# Working Out With Jeff

*I keep telling myself that I should get fit but then I see people that I know and work with starting exercise routines and they become boring and talk about 'reps' and read out the amount of calories from food wrappers as if anybody cares. A year after going to the gym and becoming experts on the amount of water they should drink per day, they are just as flabby as when they started but less interesting.*

*As I am constantly told I am too skinny, last year I paid four hundred and twenty dollars to join a gym. I attended twice. The first time for almost an hour, the second for only fifteen minutes when it dawned on me that (a) the level of fitness of the people attending the gym was inversely proportional to the level of intelligence and that (b) my instructor was not wearing anything under his Spandex bike pants and the wet semen spot would, in all probability, brush against me if I stayed there any longer.*

**From:** Jeff Peters
**Date:** Wednesday 8 April 2009 10.22am
**To:** David Thorne
**Subject:** Membership Renewal

Dear David

This is a friendly reminder to let you know your gym membership expired last week. Your membership is important to us and we would like to take this opportunity to show our appreciation by offering you a 20% discount on your membership renewal. We look forward to seeing you again soon.

All the best, Jeff Peters

......................................................................................................

**From:** David Thorne
**Date:** Wednesday 8 April 2009 1.37pm
**To:** Jeff Peters
**Subject:** Re: Membership Renewal

Dear Jeff,

Thank you for your friendly reminder and the kind offer to reduce my membership by twenty percent. I own a calculator but I could not work out how to do percentages on it so have estimated that I save around $372.10 off the normal price of $420.00 - Please confirm that this is correct and I will renew my membership immediately.

Also, do I get a Fitness First sports bag with towel and drinking bottle included in the price? I own my own legwarmers and headband.

Regards, David

**From:** Jeff Peters
**Date:** Thursday 9 April 2009 10.01am
**To:** David Thorne
**Subject:** Re: Re: Membership Renewal Due

Hello David

How did you come to that amount? Our half year membership fees are actually $460 but with the 20% discount as an existing member your renewing membership fee would be only $368 for the six months saving you almost $100 off the normal price. We're not Fitness First so do not have those bags.

Cheers, Jeff

........................................................................................

**From:** David Thorne
**Date:** Thursday 9 April 2009 10.18am
**To:** Jeff Peters
**Subject:** Re: Re: Re: Membership Renewal Due

Dear Jeff,

Do I get free shipping with that?

Regards, David

........................................................................................

**From:** Jeff Peters
**Date:** Thursday 9 April 2009 12.48pm
**To:** David Thorne
**Subject:** Re: Re: Re: Re: Membership Renewal Due

Free shipping with what? The $368 covers your membership fees for six months.

**From:** David Thorne
**Date:** Thursday 9 April 2009 2.26pm
**To:** Jeff Peters
**Subject:** Re: Re: Re: Re: Re: Membership Renewal Due

Dear Jeff,

By the power of Greyskull that's a lot of money but I admit to being in desperate need of increasing my body strength. My ten-year-old child often turns the taps off in the bathroom very tightly and I have to go several days without washing. I feel bad constantly having to ask the lady from next door to come over and loosen them for me, what with her arthritis and limited wheelchair access to my apartment.

To be honest, I originally joined your gym with full intentions of attending every few days but after waiting in vain for someone to offer me steroids, I began to suspect this was not going to happen. The realisation that I may have to exercise instead was, quite frankly, horrifying. This, and the fact one of your employees, Justin, was rather rude - telling me to "lift this", "push that" - dulled my initial enthusiasm and I stopped attending.

Regards, David

......................................................................................................

**From:** Jeff Peters
**Date:** Friday 10 April 2009 9.17am
**To:** David Thorne
**Subject:** Re: Re: Re: Re: Re: Re: Membership Renewal Due

Nobody here would offer you steroids, it's illegal and none of our staff would do this.

Justin is one of our most experienced trainers and if you found him rude while he was trying to be helpful and just doing his job then there are plenty of other gyms you could look at joining instead.

Cheers, Jeff

......................................................................................................

**From:** David Thorne
**Date:** Friday 10 April 2009 10.02am
**To:** Jeff Peters
**Subject:** Re: Re: Re: Re: Re: Re: Re: Membership Renewal Due

Dear Jeff,

Yes, I have noticed that there are many gyms in my area. I assume the low qualification requirements of fitness trainers means that there is an over supply of these buffed but essentially otherwise purposeless professionals.

I knew a guy in high school who couldn't talk very well and collected sticks, he used to call the teacher 'mum' and during recess we would give him money to dance. Then sell him sticks to get our money back. He went on to become a fitness instructor so I view gyms as kind of like those factories that provide a community service by employing people with Down Syndrome to lick stamps and pack boxes. Except with more Spandex obviously.

Regards, David

**From:** Jeff Peters
**Date:** Friday 10 April 2009 10.32am
**To:** David Thorne
**Subject:** Re: Re: Re: Re: Re: Re: Re: Re: Membership Renewal Due

Go fuck yourself.

.....................................................................................

**From:** David Thorne
**Date:** Friday 10 April 2009 11.38am
**To:** Jeff Peters
**Subject:** Re: Re: Re: Re: Re: Re: Re: Re: Re: Membership Renewal Due

Dear Jeff,

I was initially quite surprised at your response; one minute you are inviting me to renew my membership and asking me for money, the next insulting me. After doing a little research however, I understand mood swings are an expected side effect of steroid abuse. As another side effect is a reduction in penis size, this gives you understandable cause to be angry.

I've also learned Spandex contains carcinogenic properties so this does not bode well for yourself and your shiny friends. If I woke up one morning and my penis was a quarter of the size and I had testicular cancer, I would probably take my anger out on those around me as well. There are probably support groups that could help you manage your problem more effectively, and picture based books available on the subject.

Regards, David

**From:** Jeff Peters
**Date:** Friday 10 April 2009 1.04pm
**To:** David Thorne
**Subject:** Re: Re: Re: Re: Re: Re: Re: Re: Re: Re: Membership Renewal Due

DONT EMAIL ME AGAIN

---

**From:** David Thorne
**Date:** Friday 10 April 2009 1.15pm
**To:** Jeff Peters
**Subject:** Re: Re: Re: Re: Re: Re: Re: Re: Re: Re: Re: Membership Renewal Due

Okay.

---

**From:** Jeff Peters
**Date:** Friday 10 April 2009 1.25pm
**To:** David Thorne
**Subject:** Re: Re: Re: Re: Re: Re: Re: Re: Re: Re: Re: Membership Renewal Due

Is that you being a smartarse or agreeing not to email me again?

---

**From:** David Thorne
**Date:** Friday 10 April 2009 1.32pm
**To:** Jeff Peters
**Subject:** Re: Re: Re: Re: Re: Re: Re: Re: Re: Re: Re: Re: Membership Renewal Due

The middle one.

# Tom's Diary.
# A Week in the Life of a
# Creative Director

*Hello, my name is Thomas and I run a design agency. You have probably heard of me as I am known as the Design Guru of Adelaide. Everybody calls me that. You can call me Tommy though. Or the Design Guru of Adelaide if you want. Just try it and see how it sounds. No? Ok, I wasn't asking you to call me that, I was just saying most people do. It's not a problem, Tommy then. Or the Design Guru of Adelaide if you say it a few times in your head and find you prefer it because it rolls off the tongue quite well. Ok, Thomas then.*

## Monday

### 10.30am

At work early this morning as I started writing a novel last night and am keen to check if any publishers have emailed me with expressions of interest yet. I am half way through and so far it is brilliant. It's about a guy who runs a design agency during the day but at night is a karate soldier with psychic powers. And he can fly and has lots of girlfriends. I'm currently looking through photos of me for an appropriate one to use on the cover. One that says 'creative genius' but at the same time 'hey'. I will probably use one where I am sitting on a chair as it will remind people of that statue of the guy thinking called Guy Thinking. Or the one of me on the beach as my hair looks great and I am not wearing a shirt which will sell books.

## 12.30pm

Have just ordered a new MacBook Pro as my current one is almost six months old and I cannot be expected to play Solitaire at these speeds. Staff complained about the speed of theirs when they heard but I spend four to five hours each day sitting behind them watching what they do and have witnessed first hand Photoshop running fine on the Macintosh IIci they share. I just upgraded it to 8Mb a few years ago and am far too busy to be dealing with their petty issues.

## 1.30pm

Spent the last hour writing another chapter of my novel. It now spans several millenia - from the nineteenth century to the twentieth - due to the main character being immortal. Having him first jousting redcoats then, later in the novel, time travelling robots, provides contrast and a break from the parts where he has a lot of girlfriends.

## 2.30pm

Have been sitting behind the staff having brilliant ideas. I think of things all the time that are brilliant. What is it called when you are a sideways thinker? I am one of those. I usually have about ten sideways ideas per minute. I should probably sit the exam for Mensa. I am just too busy. Just this morning, while shaving my back, I thought how great it would be if my shaver had an mp3 player built in as I was in the mood for a bit of Seal and that would have made the four and a half hour process more enjoyable. I would call it the Rave'n'Shave.

### 3.30pm

Heading out for a drive shortly to buy a kite as they are a great way of meeting new friends. I have a meeting scheduled but have told the secretary that if the client comes in before I get back, to talk about me and say, "I'm surprised you managed to get an appointment with him as he is in high demand and is known as the Design Guru of Adelaide."

### 4.30pm

Got back in time for client meeting, we agreed on a package that saves me 20% on local calls so it has been a successful day. Heading home as I am exhausted and Jumper is on cable.

# Tuesday

### 12.30pm

Just got into the office as I was up late watching the movie *Jumper* and downloading the iPhone developer's kit. I played a lot of Space Invaders on my Commodore 64 when I was young and have a brilliant idea for an app that will make millions of dollars. It's a bit like Space Invaders but more like Frogger. With Braille touch screen for the blind.

## 1.30pm

Spent an hour writing another chapter of my novel. The main character now works as an international fashion model. And he has the ability to transport himself to any location on the planet as long as he has been there before.

## 2.30pm

As my creative energies are too large to be tethered to one discipline, in addition to becoming a famous author, I have decided to win Australian Idol this year.

I have my first singing lesson in half an hour. My voice is like one of those mermaids that sings to sailors as they crash onto rocks. But a man version with deeper voice and legs. Although I have the look they are after and perfect pitch and tenor, it makes sense to get a few pointers from a professional beforehand.

## 3.30pm

I've decided not to win Australian Idol this year, as I am far too busy.

## 4.00pm

Long day. Heading home after I send out an email to all staff reminding them to refer to me as the Design Guru of Adelaide and describe working with me as inspiring when they are talking about me with people at the pub or during family dinners.

# Wednesday

### 11.00am

Late one last night. Decided to go to the pub and stayed for a few drinks even though everyone I knew was leaving when I got there.

Guys are uneasy being around me with their girlfriend because they know she is thinking about me naked. Probably lifting weights or dancing. Luckily, there was a girl at the bar by herself so I sat down and talked to her about me. Surprisingly, she had not heard of me even though I am very well known and people refer to me as the Design Guru of Adelaide. Unfortunately, she had to leave before she could finish reading the news clippings about me that I keep in my pocket but she did agree to give me her mobile number, - 0123 456789 - so will ring her tonight and talk about me then.

### 1.40pm

Staff member just mentioned that eight years ago I said, "I have full body cancer with only one year to live and that's why everybody needs to work quicker." I told them that I never said that and to stop making things up. Anyway, I was talking about another guy who had cancer. He's dead now so they should show some respect.

### 2.00pm

Leaving early today to ring the girl I met last night. She will probably want to meet for a drink or come over to my place so I need to collate the photocopies of news clippings and magazine articles about me into a scrapbook for her and shampoo my chest. I also need to make a mix tape of my favourite songs. I know most of the dance moves to Disco by the Pet Shop Boys so will start slow with that before popping and locking for her with some Depeche Mode.

## Thursday

### 9.30am

Early night last night. Walked into the office talking on phone, telling client I appreciate him for saying I was the most creative and brilliant person in Australia, when the phone rang. Explained to staff that my phone is one of the new iPhones that rings while you are on a call to let you know that someone else is calling and they just haven't heard of it yet. Because their phones are old. I got cut off at the same time it rang. That's the only reason I stopped talking and looked surprised.

### 10.30am

Finishing up the final chapters of my novel. It is now set in a post-apocalyptic future where the polar ice caps have melted, water covers the planet and people live in floating towns. The main character has gills on his neck and grows tomato plants.

### 11.00am

I have a meeting to go to in an hour and need to go shopping for something nice to wear as my green trucker hat does not go with any of my canvas shoes. I should start my own t-shirt company because I have lots of brilliant ideas for t-shirt designs and people would be happy to pay upwards of two hundred dollars per shirt if they knew I had designed it. Like Ed Hardy. I would sell them online and every time someone Googled my name, it would come up with my t-shirt company and they would buy them. I should also make a website where people can buy my semen. Women would pay thousands for my semen because of my creative genes. I'm like one of those racehorses or a cow with award winning udders. I would do that if I weren't so busy.

## 4.30pm

Just got back from a four hour meeting with a potential client in regards to designing a business card for them. I'm very excited about where this could lead, as they are the eighteenth largest supplier of gravel in both the east and east-west suburbs of Adelaide. I will send them a quote in a few weeks as they take a long time to write.

I could tell they were impressed during the meeting, especially when I explained the need to incorporate cats into the design, as they continually rose, in a manner that can only be described as lengthy standing ovations, then sat down again when I kept talking. One of the female clients was very attracted to me so I spent an hour showing her colour photocopies of my Smart Roadster specs and explained what all the graphs meant. I will send her an email now and tell her my last girlfriend died of cancer so that she knows I am available, and will attach a photo of me sitting in my car. And one of me wearing jogging shorts so she knows I am athletic.

## 4.35pm

Heading home as I am exhausted both physically and mentally after two client meetings in as many months.

# Friday

## 10.30am

Walked in and had an argument with Shannon. I don't see why I have to justify myself to her. It's my business and therefore my company Visa card. I do not appreciate being questioned. Obviously there has been some kind of mistake and we have been charged $29.95 per month by teenshemale.com in error. It's not her job to ring the bank and question the purchase when I told her I would take care of it even though I am extremely busy.

## 10.35am

Have put a password on my computer. Used a random selection of 128 numbers and characters so as to make it impossible for the secretary to guess. Will not write it down anywhere in case she finds it.

## 1.30pm

Completed my novel. It is the best book ever written and will become a best seller within weeks. This will mean that I will be very busy doing promotional tours and replying to people who have written thanking me for sharing my gift so I will need to tell my staff that I will not be here as often to give them the creative guidance they rely on me for. This will be upsetting but they have to understand that I owe it to my fans to do book signing tours and appear on *Dancing with the Stars*.

To celebrate the completion of my novel, I invited the staff over to my place to listen to stories about me but they all had prior plans.

# Frogs

When I was about ten, my best friend Dominic and I would go to the creek at the end of our street and play. The creek contained thousands of tadpoles and you could easily find several frogs by lifting rocks.

We'd insert one of those thin fruit box straws into an frog's anus and blow it up like a balloon. We'd then put the frog onto the water and let go and watch it speed across the creek. Sometimes the frogs would burst as we were blowing them up. One day we threw frogs at cars driving past but were chased by a lady so we didn't do that again. On one occasion, my mother opened the freezer to find eighteen frozen frogs because I had been told that they could be frozen and then revived.

Dominic lived just five minutes from my house, with grape vines between our houses. One day he called me to come over and I left right away. As I was walking through the grapevines, I received a large push from behind and almost fell. When I turned around to confront the person who had pushed me, there was nobody there. I continued to Dominic's house and he asked where I had been because I had left my house almost four hours earlier. I have, to this day, no knowledge of where the four hours went but I think I walked through some kind of temporal distortion field, possibly to a far off future where I met my soul mate, grew old together and was then given the choice after she died to return to my own time, the moment I left, with no memory of my future life. This is obviously the most likely explanation.

A couple of years ago I was in the area with my son and we went to the creek but there were no frogs or tadpoles in it. This could be because they have all died out from pollution over the years but I prefer to think that they are fine and remembered me through some form of inherited group memory and hid. We did find a shopping trolley though which entertained my son for about an hour so that was good.

I thought I would have a lot more to write about frogs but I'm bored already.

## Frog Facts

The Brazilian Jungle Frog can mimic human speech and grows to the size of a small child.

Frozen frogs make a healthy and fun addition to any kid's school lunch box.

When blended, frogs make an excellent energy drink which contains 92% of reccomended daily vitamin intake.

While frogs have a varied diet, which includes nuts and corn, their favourite meal is the cheese quesadilla from Applebee's for $6.69.

Frogs have excellent reception and can be used in place of your standard television aerial.

Placed between tissue paper and under heavy books for a few weeks, a dried frog makes a stunning broach.

**Blockbuster Video Pty Ltd**
555 Portrush Rd Glenunga SA 5064
**Tel** (08) 8338 0053
**Fax** (08) 8338 0048
www.blockbuster.com.au
ABN 992 002 682

4.11.2009

Dear Mr Thorne,

I am writing to advise that movies borrowed on the 14th of October
are now three weeks overdue and have accumulated fees of $82.
Please return the following movies before they gain further fees.

002190582 Journey to the Centre of the Earth
003103119 Logans Run
008629103 Harold and Kumar Escape from Guantanamo Bay
000721082 Waterworld

Kind regards,
Megan

Megan Roberts
Store Manager

Blockbuster Video Pty Ltd
555 Portrush Rd Glenunga SA 5064
Tel (08) 8338 0053
megan.roberts@blockbuster.com.au
www.blockbuster.com.au

# Blockbuster

*I find it annoying to pay late fees on movies and I am too lazy to return them on time, which leaves complaining about it. I used to know a guy named Matthew who sold me copies of the latest movies for five dollars, but they were all recorded by someone in a cinema with what appeared to be a low resolution web cam and epilepsy. Several times during each movie, the person would shift positions or have people walk past in front or film the back of the chair in front of them. Matthew claimed he didn't know the quality before he got them but during one of the movies, the person filming answered his phone and said, "Hello Matthew speaking." When I mentioned this to Matthew, he stopped selling me movies.*

**From:** David Thorne
**Date:** Sunday 8 November 2009 2.16pm
**To:** Megan Roberts
**Subject:** DVDs

Dear Megan,

Thank you for your letter regarding overdue fees. As all four movies were modern cinematic masterpieces, your assumption that I would wish to retain them in my possession is understandable, but incorrect. Please check your records as these movies were returned, on time, over three weeks ago. I remember driving there and having my offspring run them in due to the fact that I was wearing shorts and did not want the girl behind the counter to see my white hairy legs.

Regards, David

**From:** Megan Roberts
**Date:** Monday 9 November 2009 11.09am
**To:** David Thorne
**Subject:** Re: DVDs

Hi David.

Our computer system indicates otherwise. Please recheck and get back to me.

Kind regards, Megan

**From:** David Thorne
**Date:** Monday 9 November 2009 11.36am
**To:** Megan Roberts
**Subject:** Re: Re: DVDs

Dear Megan,

Yes, they are definitely white and hairy. Viewed from the knees down, the similarity to two large albino caterpillars in parallel formation is frightening. People who knew what the word meant might describe them as 'piliferous', although there is something quite sexy about that word so perhaps they wouldn't.

Regards, David.

. . . . . . . . . . . . . . . . . . . . . . . . . . . . . . . . . . . . . . . . . . . . . . . . . . . . . . . . . . . . . . . . . . . . . . . . . . . . . . . .

**From:** Megan Roberts
**Date:** Monday 9 November 2009 1.44pm
**To:** David Thorne
**Subject:** Re: Re: Re: DVDs

Hi David

No I mean our records indicate that the DVDs have not been
returned. Please check and return as soon as possible.

Kind regards, Megan

. . . . . . . . . . . . . . . . . . . . . . . . . . . . . . . . . . . . . . . . . . . . . . . . . . . . . . . . . . . . . . . . . . . . . . . . . . . . . . . .

**From:** David Thorne
**Date:** Monday 9 November 2009 4.19pm
**To:** Megan Roberts
**Subject:** Re: Re: Re: Re: DVDs

Dear Megan,

With the possible exception of *Harold and Kumar Escape from
Guantanamo Bay*, the movies were not worth watching let alone
stealing.

In *Logan's Run*, for example, the computer crashed at the end
when presented with conflicting facts and blew up destroying
the entire city. When my computer crashes, I carry on a little bit
and have a cigarette while it is rebooting. I don't have to search

179

through rubble for my loved ones. The same programmers probably designed the Blockbuster 'returned or not' database.

Also, while one would assume the title *Journey to the Centre of the Earth* to be a metaphor, the movie was actually set in the centre of the earth which, being a solid core of iron with temperatures exceeding 4300° Celsius and pressures of 3900 tons per square centimetre, does not seem very likely.

*Waterworld* was actually pretty good though. My favourite bit was when Kevin Costner negotiated for peace, ending the war between fish and mankind moments before the whale army attacked.

Regards, David.

....................................................................................................

**From:** Megan Roberts
**Date:** Tuesday 10 November 2009 3.57pm
**To:** David Thorne
**Subject:** Re: Re: Re: Re: Re: DVDs

David

The DVDs are listed as not returned. If you cant locate the DVDs, you will be charged for the replacement cost.

Megan

**From:** David Thorne
**Date:** Tuesday 10 November 2009 5.12pm
**To:** Megan Roberts
**Subject:** Re: Re: Re: Re: Re: Re: DVDs

Dear Megan,

I have checked pricing at the DVD Warehouse and the cost of replacing your lost movies with new ones is as follows:

*Harold and Kumar Escape from Guantanamo Bay* $7.95
*Waterworld* $4.95
*Journey to the Centre of the Earth* $9.95
*Logan's Run* $12.95

I have no idea why Logan's Run is the most expensive of the four movies. Have you seen it? The entire premise comprised of living a utopian and carefree lifestyle with only three drawbacks - wearing jumpsuits, living in what looks like a giant shopping centre, and not being allowed to live past thirty. Possibly because they didn't want a bunch of old people hanging around complaining about their arthritis while they were attempting to relax at the shopping centre in their jumpsuits and trying not to think about the computer crashing.

I was forced to do volunteer work at an aged care hospital recently. Footage of these people during Tuesday night line-dancing could be used as an advertisement for the Logan's Run solution. The only good aspect of working there was that I halved their medication and pocketed what was left over. I explained the computer listed that as their dose and that they were welcome to check - knowing their abject fear of anything produced after the eighteenth century would prevent them from doing so.

I also swapped my Sanyo fourteen inch portable television for their Panasonic wide screen plasma while they were sleeping - explaining that it had always been that way and their senility was simply playing up due to the reduced dosage of drugs.

Regards, David.

........................................................................................

**From:** Megan Roberts
**Date:** Wednesday 11 November 2009 1.21pm
**To:** David Thorne
**Subject:** Re: Re: Re: Re: Re: Re: DVDs

David

I haven't seen those movies. I prefer romantic comedies. If you have the movies we can't rent them so we lose money and the fees are based on what we would have made from renting them and we also have to purchase movies through our suppliers not from DVD Warehouse.

Megan

**From:** David Thorne
**Date:** Wednesday 11 November 2009 3.28pm
**To:** Megan Roberts
**Subject:** Re: Re: Re: Re: Re: Re: Re: Re: DVDs

Dear Megan,

I too am a fan of romantic comedies. Perhaps we could watch one together. I have a new Panasonic wide screen plasma.

My favourite romantic comedy is *Transformers*, although it did not contain enough robots or explosions in my opinion. Recently, I was tricked into watching The Notebook, which was about geese. Lots of geese. It also had something to do with an old lady who conveniently lost her memory so she could not remember being a whore throughout the entire film. I don't recall a lot of it, as I was too busy being cross about watching it. In a utopian future society she would have been hunted down and killed at thirty.

In regards to the late fees, I understand the amount is based on what you lose by not being able to rent the movies out. You probably had people lined up around the block waiting to rent *Logan's Run*.

For eighty two dollars however, I could have purchased six copies of it from DVD Warehouse or, as I have heard he is a bit strapped for cash, had Kevin Costner visit my house and re-enact key scenes from *Waterworld* in the bathroom.

Regards, David

**From:** Megan Roberts
**Date:** Thursday 12 November 2009 3.16pm
**To:** David Thorne
**Subject:** Re: Re: Re: Re: Re: Re: Re: Re: Re: DVDs

Restocking fees are:

002190382 *Journey to the Centre of the Earth* $9.30
003103119 *Logans Run* $7.90
008629103 *Harold and Kumar Escape from Guantanamo Bay* $6.30
000721082 *Waterworld* $5.70

Total: $29.20 - I have deleted your late fees and noted on the computer that the amount owed is for the replacement movies not fees.

Kind regards, Megan

⋯⋯⋯⋯⋯⋯⋯⋯⋯⋯⋯⋯⋯⋯⋯⋯⋯⋯⋯⋯⋯⋯⋯⋯⋯⋯⋯⋯⋯⋯⋯⋯⋯⋯⋯⋯

**From:** David Thorne
**Date:** Thursday 12 November 2009 7.42pm
**To:** Megan Roberts
**Subject:** Re: Re: Re: Re: Re: Re: Re: Re: Re: Re: DVDs

Dear Megan,

The prices seem reasonable. I do not, however, require two copies.

Regards, David

**From:** Megan Roberts
**Date:** Friday 13 November 2009 12.51pm
**To:** David Thorne
**Subject:** Re: Re: Re: Re: Re: Re: Re: Re: Re: Re: Re: DVDs

The $29.20 is the cost of the replacement DVDs for the store.

What do you mean by 2 copies? Do you have the movies?

........................................................................................

**From:** David Thorne
**Date:** Friday 13 November 2009 1.15pm
**To:** Megan Roberts
**Subject:** Re: Re: Re: Re: Re: Re: Re: Re: Re: Re: Re: Re: DVDs

Dear Megan,

Yes, apparently they were on top of my fridge the whole time. I have a blind spot that prevents me from seeing this area of the kitchen as it's where I keep my pile of unpaid bills. As you have already waived the late fees, I will drop the movies off tonight and we'll call it even.

Regards, David

........................................................................................

**From:** Megan Roberts
**Date:** Friday 13 November 2009 2.33pm
**To:** David Thorne
**Subject:** Re: Re: Re: Re: Re: Re: Re: Re: Re: Re: Re: Re: Re: DVDs

Okay.

# Skye Cargan. Stuntman.

Hello, my name is Skye Cargan and I'm Australia's most extreme stunt man to the awesomest max. If you have an event that you need a show for, please contact me and I will do you a good price. I will be famous soon and the price will go up so be quick.

My most recent stunts include running on the concrete at the swimming pool, flicking the light switch on and off repeatedly, sitting too close to the television, and lighting myself on fire - if you hold a gas lighter in your fist with the button depressed, then spark it, the gas ignites for a couple of seconds. My sister said it was the best stunt she has ever seen. I'm currently preparing for my latest stunt in which I intend to eat a hotdog and go swimming without waiting thirty minutes.

I've written my own theme song which I sing while I am doing my stunts:

*Skye Cargan to the Extreme.* By Skye Cargan.

It's Skye Cargan, being extreme to the awesomest max!

Did you see what he just he did? No?

Pity because it was amazing!

Woh!

# Barnesyfan67

Hello, my name is Joanne and my favourite hobbies are laughing in the mirror and sitting in my favorite chair at the window. I have venetian blinds so I can see out but people can't see in. If I turn the lights out, I can sit there the whole night and nobody knows I am watching.

I have a poster of a dolphin in my bedroom and a picture of a tiger on my quilt. I call the tiger Mishka. Sometimes I lie on my quilt and pat him and tell him my problems.

My last boyfriend, Darren, installed an Audio 4 sound system in my Datsun. It has an input plug so that you can play songs from your iPod. I don't own an iPod but if I had a friend with an iPod, I would be like, "Hey girlfriend, lets play music from your iPod through my stereo, do you have a N33 adapter cable?" and they would, and we'd listen to Keith Urban on the way to Target. Darren also bought me a Teac television from Cash Converters. It was ninety dollars but he talked them down to seventy-five and got two VHS videos with it - *Splash* and *Cannonball Run*.

Darren and I were going to be married but his mother told me he died in a fire. Why did he have to rescue those children from a burning apartment? I have a mobile phone tower in my backyard.

# 1000 Characters

*Posting in Internet forums can be entertaining but there's often a limit of one-thousand characters per post. As I'm often writing something insensitive simply to evoke an outraged response, each post (including punctuation, spaces, introduction, proposal, argument, and punch line) needs to contained within a single small paragraph. When I was fourteen, I was given the task of drowning kittens by my girlfriend's mother. I half-filled a large laundry sink with room temperature water and held the eight kittens under. As each kitten stopped struggling and sank to the bottom, it turned and 'snuggled' to the previous kitten. After I was done, I put them in a garbage bag and was carrying it out when I heard a tiny mew. Opening the bag, I discovered one of the kittens had survived. So I drowned it again. And that is an exact one thousand.*

## Sharks

My offspring wanted scuba gear for his birthday. That's all he wanted. I'm not letting him swim off to be mistaken for a baby seal by a great white and I'm not going in there with him to be mistaken for an old skinny seal by a great white. When I explained that scuba gear is for the sea and he, being such a small human, would be mistaken for a baby seal by a great white, he added 'speargun' to his birthday list.

## Cats

I agreed to look after a friend's cat for the week. My place has a glass atrium that goes through two levels and I have put the cat in there with enough food and water to last the week. It's glaring at me as I type and I can tell it would like to kill me. If I knew I could get a perfect replacement cat, I'd kill this one and replace it at the end of the week. The simplest way would be to drop heavy items on it from the upstairs bedroom although I have enough basic engineering knowledge to build some form of spear. If the atrium was waterproof, I could flood it with water. It wouldn't have to be that deep, just deeper than the cat. I don't know how long cats can swim but I doubt it's capable of keeping it up for a whole week. If so, I could always try dropping things on it as well. I've read that drowning is one of the most peaceful ways to die so really it would be a win-win situation for both the cat and me.

## Riddick

While watching the movie *Chronicles of Riddick* together last night, my offspring stated that he wished Riddick was his dad. When I asked why, he replied that Riddick is good looking, has muscles and is a good fighter. I told him that I wished Matthew (his arch-enemy at school) was my son because he's better at maths and has cool hair.

## Tampons

My offspring's birthday is next week. When he was seven, I told him to draw pictures of what he wanted for his birthday as a visual list. When I enquired as to one image (which I first took to be a box of coloured crayons), I deciphered his explanations as it being tampons. In particular, the multicoloured brand. His only references were adverts featuring a girl jumping out of a window onto a tree which lowered her into a BMW convertible full of friends, an electric green street racing car with black flames and the ability to do a single-handed handstand star-jump on a dance machine to crowd applause. I bought him a box and figured he would work it out. Yesterday I asked him what he wants for his birthday and he replied, 'Not tampons'.

## Girls That Have Said No Part 1

While working at a horse riding camp several years ago, I spent a good twenty minutes explaining to a group, which consisted of twelve children and their young teacher, the importance of horse safety before walking behind a horse and being kicked in the head. I recall walking in a zigzag back to the house with the muffled sounds of children screaming in the background before collapsing and waking up in hospital. While I was there, with a fractured skull, the teacher bought me in a get well soon card signed by all the children so I asked her out but she said no.

## Anhus Street

A street I drive past every day is called Anhus Street and it's quite distracting. Every few weeks, someone (I am assuming a kid) spraypaints out the 'h' making it read Anus and a few days later, someone (I'm assuming an elderly street resident) paints the 'h' back in. If I were boss of the world, I'd change the street name legally to Anus Street to annoy them both.

## Dreams

I hate it when people state, "I had a weird dream last night..." I don't care, it didn't really happen. Just because you dreamt it doesn't make it interesting to anyone. A woman named Brooke once told me about a dream she had, and it went on for twenty minutes. That's nineteen minutes and sixty seconds longer than

I can pretend to care about anything that didn't actually happen. Another time, she told me about a dream her auntie had, so not only was I listening to something that didn't really happen, I was listening to something that didn't really happen to someone I didn't know. Her statement, "If you cared one bit about me, you'd be interested in my dreams," is probably correct.

## Superconductors

If you take the temperature of a superconductor down to absolute zero (around minus 273.1 centigrade), it ignores gravity and floats. This is a scientific fact and you are welcome to check. My offspring asked why we couldn't freeze a car to -273C and fly in it, and I explained that the car would neutralise gravity, not reverse it, and the weight of the people in it would make it sink. Also, heat rises so -273C should really sink unless it was in a vacuum, which means we wouldn't be able to breathe or hear the stereo. You would also need to rug up well.

## Girls That Have Said No Part 2

When I was ten or so, my sister often had friends staying over. I would dress in ninja gear and wriggle into her bedroom to listen to their conversations. Some were educational, most were inane. A few months ago, I was standing in a cd store and a girl came up to me and asked, "Are you David?" to which I replied, "It depends" (and immediately regretted as I knew that if she asked me, 'Depends on what', I had nothing). "Depends on what?" she asked and I replied, "On whether it is on or off the record, I've been misquoted by you people before." and she looked at me oddly before stating she had been a friend of my sister and asked, "Are you still annoying?" so I asked her if she still "Squeezed her nipples while thinking about kissing Michael Wilson." After a long pause, I asked her out but she said no.

## Girls That Have Said No Part 3

At the local swimming pool canteen, not realising until afterwards that my penis was caught in the elastic of my swimming shorts with the tip sticking out, I purchased a packet of Twisties and a can of Coke before asking out the girl who served me but she said no.

## Parking spot

A few weeks ago, some guy in a shitty BMW parked in my 'reserved and paid for' parking spot. I printed out an A4 (Helvetica Demi Bold 12pt) note stating that it was a paid for parking spot and left it under his wiper blade. He parked there again the next day so I printed out an A3 (helvetica black 42pt) sign stating, "Reserved Parking, Do not park here," and used spray adhesive to mount it on the wall in front of my spot. He parked in my spot again the next day so I printed out an A2 poster (Helvetica Black, 92pt, reversed) with the words, "Stop parking in my spot, dickhead," and applied it with spray adhesive to his windscreen - ensuring (as per instructions) I sprayed both materials to be bonded. I'm too scared to park in my spot, in case he retaliates, but he hasn't parked there since so I'll class this as a draw and find a new spot.

## Girls That Have Said No Part 4

A new girl started working at the petrol station near my place last week and I asked her if she had a carfor. She asked, "what's a carfor?" and I replied, "Driving around in when I'm not paying ninety two dollars to feed it." After admonishing her for the poor choice of CDs they sold on the counter, I asked her out but she said no.

## Confession

When I was about thirteen, I'd wag school and go to a Christian bookstore called The Open Book. It covered two levels with a second-hand section in the basement. Selecting a dozen or so expensive theological volumes from the shelves, I'd put them in my school bag, then go downstairs to the basement where they'd purchase the books from me for half the listed price. I did this twice a week for several months but somehow they never caught on. I was saving for a motorbike and bought a Suzuki Katana. The Open Book went broke a year later so it worked out well for everyone.

## eBay

I bought a dinosaur's tooth fossil recently, with a certificate of authenticity, as it's something I've always wanted. There's a quarry a short drive away that my offspring and I explore sometimes. When we went there last, I suggested we dig for fossils and I 'discovered' the dinosaur tooth - thinking it would be a big deal to him - but he stated, "No, it's just a rock." When I stated that I was positive that it is was a Saurischian tooth from the Mesozoic era, he replied that I had, "Made that up," and for me to "Throw it away." I can't prove to him that it is a real dinosaur tooth without divulging I purchased it and he is never seeing the invoice, as I would have to explain why I didn't buy a Playstation instead. Occasionally he picks it up and gives me a disdaining look. Also, I bought some NASA mission badges a while back off eBay. He asked me if they had been in space and when I admitted they hadn't, he stated, "Well that's just weak then."

# Professional Photography Tips With Thomas

*Hello, my name is Thomas and I'm a professional photographer because I bought a digital camera.*

**Tip 1** *How to become a professional photographer*

Buy a digital camera.

**Tip 2** *Tricks of the trade*

Somewhere on the camera, there will be a button or dial marked 'A', this does not stand for 'Automatic' as some amateurs think, but 'Awesome'. Leave it on this all the time.

**Tip 3** *Photography courses*

There is no need for even a basic photography course because once you buy a digital camera you will be a professional photographer like me. Not as good as me though.

**Tip 4** *Subject Matter*

Yes it does. Don't take photos of schoolgirls from your car as the fine is $360 and a year's probation.

Sunset from my rooftop.

View of city from my rooftop.

The plant on my rooftop.

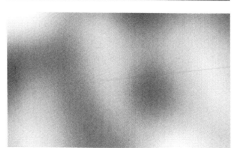

Some people that once came to visit me on my rooftop. Or my toes.

195

# Flight Commander

*Thank you for joining us today and congratulations on your recent successful mission aboard Discovery. Could you explain to us what it was like to be in space?*

Yes, I can. It was a lot smaller than I expected. I used to try to take in the fact that earth is spinning around a tiny sun which is just one of billions in a tiny cluster that makes up just a bit of our milky way which is one of billions of galaxies with billions of billions of kilometres between them and I would get a massive headache and an overwhelming feeling of insignificance with bouts of depression that ultimately led to the breakdown of my third marriage, but when you get up there, you realise there's not that much to it.

*How long does it take to reach your mission destination?*

Good question. Contrary to popular belief, distances in space are pretty close, rockets are seriously fast so it only takes about 12 minutes to get to the moon and an hour or so to Mars. It was assumed the distances were greater because of our mistaken calculations in regards to the size of objects in space. The moon for example was thought to be 384,633 kilometres away due to the calculation of it having a radius of 3476 kilometres but in fact it is only 16 kilometres up with a radius of 2.3 kilometres. I myself walked the complete circumference of the moon in under an hour and that included stopping often to look at interesting rocks. If I throw one of the rocks out into space it will travel through the void for eternity. I usually do this three or four hundred times each visit. Sometimes I spit on the rocks first, knowing my DNA may travel to another world countless light years away and fertilise a new beginning for mankind.

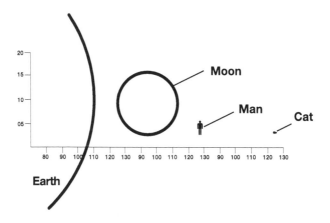

*Could you explain the functions of your suit?*

Yes, the suits are pretty cool, aren't they? They may look uncomfortable but are actually like wearing a quilt and can be put on or taken off in under 30 seconds. I often wear mine around the house when I am ironing, mowing the lawn, or popping down to the shops to get some milk. The controls on the front may seem complicated but simply control the bass, treble and volume of the built in mp3 player.

*How do you prepare for each mission takeoff?*

We try to get a good sleep the night before, making sure everything is packed and we haven't forgotten anything. Once the ignition spark hits 20 tons of solid rocket fuel, we can't turn around and go to the shop. During one mission, nobody remembered to bring cigarettes so everyone was bitching and grumpy - I had a packet in my suit but I had to hide them and only smoke in the toilet or everyone would have wanted one. Music is also very important, we strap in, run a pre launch flight check then press the ignition switch hitting us with 9000G of thrust at exactly 12 seconds into the Linkin Park track *With You* which is fed at full volume through our helmet speakers.

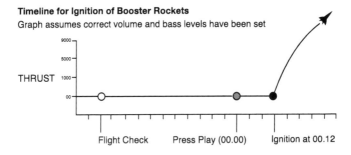

**Timeline for Ignition of Booster Rockets**
Graph assumes correct volume and bass levels have been set

*As Commander, you must rely on a dedicated and highly skilled crew to ensure each successful mission.*

You'd assume that wouldn't you? You'd think that a team would support their commander and encourage his leadership and support his decisions wouldn't you. You'd expect there to be no bickering or saying stuff behind people's backs wouldn't you?

Good teamwork comes from listening to your commander, that's why there are ranks. Some people just don't understand that there is no I in team. I tell them that the word team stands for *Terrifically Exciting Aims Met* and had T-Shirts made, but they didn't wear them..

*Thank you, Commander, for taking the time out of your busy schedule to come and talk to us today. Is there any last message you would like to give to our students?*

No problem, I wasn't doing much today. Well if there was one message I would like to give to the kids of today, it would be not to do drugs. They may seem fun at the time and yes, they enhance sex and make music sound better, but they can be expensive unless you know the right people so you are better off buying books and pens and stuff. Space may be big but it's nowhere near as big as your potential.

# CCTV
# A busy day in the design studio.

**9.40AM**
Shannon arrives and looks out the window.

**11.58AM**
Shannon gets petty cash.

**12.01PM**
Shannon pops out to "get lunch and do some things."

**1.50PM**
Shannon looks out window.

**4.11PM**
Thomas leaves for meeting with himself.

**4.12PM**
Shannon diverts phone upstairs as she has to leave to "do some stuff".

STEVENSON
STRATA MANAGEMENT

Office
178 Fullarton Road
Dulwich, South Australia 5065

Postal Address
P.O. Box 3115
Kent Town, South Australia 5071

Phone
T 08 8267 2900
F 08 8364 1795

Accounts Department Contact
Fax 08 8431 8450

Whitlow Management Services Pty Ltd
of Whitlow Strata Unit Trust
trading as Whitlow Strata Management

ABN 31 443 570 729

18th May, 2009

Mr David Thorne

Adelaide, South Australia

Dear Mr Thorne,

It has come to our attention through complaints by other tenants in your building that you have a dog at the premises. Under the agreement you signed as part of the Strata, animals are not permitted.

Please call me or email me at hel████████████h.com.au to discuss this matter as soon as possible.

Yours Sincerely,

Helen Bailey

# Strata Agreement

*If I had a large backyard, I'd probably have about a thousand pets but I can't have any due to my Strata agreement and the fact that pets need to be fed and taken for walks and I'm too lazy for that. There's a park across the road from my apartment but the last time I went there, I was offered fifty dollars by an old guy wearing clogs to provide a sexual act - which was flattering but I told him I was late for a meeting otherwise I would. Which was a lie as I think I just played Unreal Tournament the rest of that day. I'm not getting on my knees in a public toilet and sucking off an old guy wearing clogs for anything less than seventy-five.*

*I did have a goldfish named (posthumously) Stinky who lived in a glass vase with a plant. My offspring won him at the Royal Adelaide Show by tossing three rings onto milk bottles. We couldn't go on any rides after that because we had a goldfish. When Stinky died, I figured it would be nice to leave him in the vase so that his body would break down and fertilise the plant, but after just a few weeks, the smell was so terrible I couldn't be in the apartment without a towel wrapped around my face, so I took him to work and hid him in Simon's desk instead.*

**From:** David Thorne
**Date:** Thursday 21 May 2009 10.16am
**To:** Helen Bailey
**Subject:** Pets in the building

Dear Helen,

I have received your letter concerning pets in my apartment.

I understand having dogs in the apartment is a violation of the agreement due to the comfort and wellbeing of my neighbours and I am currently soundproofing my apartment with egg cartons as I realise my dogs can cause quite a bit of noise.

Especially during feeding time when I release live rabbits.

Regards, David

......................................................................................................

**From:** Helen Bailey
**Date:** Thursday 21 May 2009 11.18am
**To:** David Thorne
**Subject:** Re: Pets in the building

Hello David

I wish to remind you that the agreement states that no animals are allowed in the building regardless of if your apartment is soundproof.

How many dogs do you have at the premises?

Helen

**From:** David Thorne
**Date:** Thursday 21 May 2009 1.52pm
**To:** Helen Bailey
**Subject:** Re: Re: Pets in the building

Dear Helen,

I currently only have eight dogs but one is expecting puppies. I'm hoping for a litter of ten as this is the number required to participate in dog sled racing. I've read every Jack London novel in preparation and have constructed my own sled from timber borrowed from the construction site across the road during the night.

I have devised a plan which I feel will ensure me taking first place in the next national dog sled championships: For the first year of their lives, I intend to chase the puppies around the apartment while yelling "Mush!" and hitting saucepan lids together. I estimate the soundproofing of my apartment should block out 60% of the noise, and the dogs will learn to associate the word mush with great fear so when they hear it on race day, the panic and released adrenaline will spur them on to being winners.

I'm so confident of this plan that I intend to sell my furniture the day before the race and bet the proceeds on coming first.

Regards, David

**From:** Helen Bailey
**Date:** Friday 22 May 2009 9.43am
**To:** David Thorne
**Subject:** Re: Re: Re: Pets in the building

David,

Do you have pets in the apartment or not?

Helen

........................................................................................

**From:** David Thorne
**Date:** Friday 22 May 2009 11.27am
**To:** Helen Bailey
**Subject:** Re: Re: Re: Re: Pets in the building

Dear Helen,

No. The ducks in the bathroom are not mine.

The noise which my neighbours mistook for a dog in the apartment is just a looping tape of dogs barking I play while I am at work to deter burglars from breaking in and stealing my Tupperware. I need it to keep food fresh. I once ate leftover Chinese that had been kept in an unsealed container and I experienced complete awareness. I tried it again the next night but only experienced chest pains and diarrhea.

Regards, David

**From:** Helen Bailey
**Date:** Friday 22 May 2009 1.46pm
**To:** David Thorne
**Subject:** Re: Re: Re: Re: Re: Pets in the building

Hello David

You can't play sounds of dogs or any noise at a volume that disturbs others. I'm sure you can appreciate that these rules are for the benefit of all residents of the building. Fish are fine. You cannot have ducks in the apartment. If it was small birds that would be ok.

Helen

---

**From:** David Thorne
**Date:** Friday 22 May 2009 2.18pm
**To:** Helen Bailey
**Subject:** Re: Re: Re: Re: Re: Re: Pets in the building

Dear Helen,

They're very small ducks.

Regards, David

---

**From:** Helen Bailey
**Date:** Friday 22 May 2009 4.06pm
**To:** David Thorne
**Subject:** Re: Re: Re: Re: Re: Re: Re: Pets in the building

David, under section 4 of the Strata Residency Agreement it states you cannot have pets. You agreed to these rules when you signed the forms. These rules are set out to benefit everyone in the building including you. Do you have a telephone number I can call you on to discuss?

Helen

........................................................................................

**From:** David Thorne
**Date:** Friday 22 May 2009 5.02pm
**To:** Helen Bailey
**Subject:** Re: Re: Re: Re: Re: Re: Re: Re: Pets in the building

Dear Helen,

The ducks will no doubt be flying south for the winter soon so it will not be an issue. It's probably for the best, as they are not getting along well with my seventeen cats.

Regards, David

........................................................................................

**From:** Helen Bailey
**Date:** Monday 25 May 2009 9.22am
**To:** David Thorne
**Subject:** Re: Re: Re: Re: Re: Re: Re: Re: Re: Pets in the building

David, I am just going to write on the forms that we have investigated and you do not have any pets.

Helen

# New Zealand

Hello, my name is Josh and I live in Wellington, the capital of New Zealand. When I grow up, I want to drive the village car. My plan is to drive to the neighbouring village in the middle of the night and steal their fire. The residents of Wellington will probably build a mud statue in my honour like they did for my uncle Robert when he caught a pig.

Every day, I play the national sport of *Throw a Stick at a Sheep* in which you throw a stick at a sheep. When I'm not playing *Throw a Stick at A Sheep*, I play a game called *Find Where the Stick Went*.

If I were a sheep, I'd pick up one of the sticks and write something in the dirt and become famous. I would be rich and could buy a Porsche.

Every seventy-four days - when it's my turn to wear the village shoes - I go for a hike, enjoying the feeling of not having sheep droppings between my toes, and climb a hill to sit at the top and sing. My favourite song is called Kahadanhibrakahana, which, roughly translated from Maori, means 'I am sitting on a hill'. As I share a bedroom with seventeen siblings, this solitude is something I look forward to. Sometimes I play *Throw a Stick at a Sheep* but usually I just masturbate. I saw a helicopter once.

**South Australia Police**

"Leading the way to a safer community"

BOX 1539 GPO, ADELAIDE SA 5001
TELEPHONE: 8207 5000
A.B.N. 93 799 021 552

Your Ref
Our Ref    PO8 2010/7281
Enquiries
Telephone
Facsimile

25 February 2010

Mr David Thorne
PO Box 10476
ADELAIDE BC SOUTH AUSTRALIA 5000

Dear Mr Thorne

I am writing concerning content you currently have included on the website www.27bslash6.com condoning the use of drugs. While I understand that you may have been trying to be funny, the solicitation of drugs for the intention of selling or for personal use is a criminal offence under South Australian law.

I advise you to remove the content within 48 hours receipt of this letter.

I can be contacted on (08 or emailed at ████████████ice.sa.gov.au. I am on duty all day this week from 10am to 6pm if you have any questions.

Yours sincerely

Michael HARDING
Acting officer in charge
E-Crime Section
SOUTH AUSTRALIAN POLICE

Ph (08) ████████

# South Australian Police. Protecting society from blogs.

*Having written an article where I stated that I wished to purchase drugs and sell them at a profit, I was contacted by SA Police who pointed out that it is a criminal offence to solicit money with the intent to purchase drugs and sell them at a profit. As such, I have amended the article accordingly.*

**From**: David Thorne
**Date**: Friday 26 February 2010 8.12pm
**To**: Michael Harding
**Subject**: Censorship

Dear Michael,

Thank you for your letter. At no time have I condoned the use of drugs, I simply stated that I wish to purchase and sell them at a profit. I do however understand the importance of censorship; without enforced guidance, we'd all have to exercise our own discretion.

Regards, David

**From**: Michael Harding
**Date**: Saturday 27 February 2010 10.27am
**To**: David Thorne
**Subject**: Re: Censorship

David, your disrespect for authority doesn't change the fact that soliciting money for the purpose of purchasing and selling drugs is a criminal offence under South Australian law. I advise you to remove the article and I will check that you have done so by 5pm tomorrow.

Yours sincerely, Michael Harding

........................................................................................................

**From**: David Thorne
**Date**: Saturday 27 February 2010 10.44am
**To**: Michael Harding
**Subject**: Re: Re: Censorship

Dear Michael,

Despite your assumption, I have the highest amount of respect for authority. I actually applied to become a police officer but failed the IQ test when I arrived on time at the correct building.

I considered applying again, as protecting the community from burglars, murderers and blogs must be very fulfilling, but I've heard they test for drugs.

Regards, David

**From:** Michael Harding
**Date:** Saturday 27 February 2010 2.09pm
**To:** David Thorne
**Subject:** Re: Re: Re: Censorship

You might not take this seriously but I can assure you we do. You have until 5pm tomorrow to remove the article.

................................................................................

**From:** David Thorne
**Date:** Saturday 27 February 2010 3.18pm
**To:** Michael Harding
**Subject:** Re: Re: Re: Re: Censorship

Dear Michael,

I do take the matter seriously and will attempt to facilitate your request despite the fact that I am extremely busy this weekend. I need to bury the two dead backpackers I have in my spare room as the smell is attracting cats.

It's a large job as one of the backpackers is American and will require a hole several sizes larger than normal. On the plus side, the other is from England, which means no dental records. I'll probably just let the children out for a game of 'best digger gets food this week' - I'm sick of hearing, "I want my parents," and, "Please don't lock me in the spare room again, it smells funny," but many hands, no matter how small, make light work.

Also, I was watching *Crime Stoppers* last night and was wondering if you need anyone to play the perpetrators in crime re-enactments? I'd prefer to play either a black professor or an Asian bus driver.

Regards, David

**From**: Michael Harding
**Date**: Sunday 28 February 2010 10.26am
**To**: David Thorne
**Subject**: Re: Re: Re: Re: Re: Censorship

I'd suggest using the time you have left to delete the page rather than writing about dead backpackers and abducted children. Both of which are serious matters. I will be filing an order at 5PM today under the e-crimes act of 2006 to have the website suspended if the page is not deleted.

......................................................................................

**From**: David Thorne
**Date**: Sunday 28 February 2010 5.01pm
**To**: Michael Harding
**Subject**: Re: Re: Re: Re: Re: Re: Censorship

Dear Mike,

My apologies for not getting back to you earlier, I was busy torching my vehicle. Did you know that if you report it stolen, the insurance company buys you a new one? I do this every eleven months as it saves having to pay for an annual service.

I do not really have dead backpackers or abducted children in my spare room. There's no space in there due to the meth lab.

Rather than deleting the article, I have replaced all references to drugs. I trust this resolves the matter.

Regards, David

......................................................................................

**From**: Michael Harding
**Date**: Sunday 28 February 2010 5.17pm
**To**: David Thorne
**Subject**: Re: Re: Re: Re: Re: Re: Re: Censorship

That's fine.

# Investment Opportunity

**Business Plan**

$5120.00 in raised capital is required. $5000.00 of which is to purchase cats. The extra $120.00 will go towards purchasing a metal briefcase like you see in movies to put the cats in. I will then sell the cats at a profit.

I once paid twenty dollars for a cat which had almost no effect. Years later, I was told by the person who sold it to me that it was actually a dried up raisin they had found in the couch and had needed the money for cigarettes. This indicates not only a ready and willing market, but also a markup of 82,432% on initial investment.

**Return on Investment**

# Hello, my name is Jason and I own a MacBook Pro.

*Do you own a Macbook Pro? It's ok if you don't own a MacBook Pro because MacBook Pro's are only for creative people. People sometimes ask me, "Is that a MacBook Pro?" to which I reply, "Yes it is, because I'm creative."*

### Letter to Steve Jobs

Dear Steve,

Thankyou for inventing the MacBook Pro. On the next model, could you please write the word 'Pro' in bold?

P.S. I watched *Pirates of Silicon Valley* the other night and thought you were a bit mean to your girlfriend. Apart from that you were really cool. I have a poster of you on my wall.

Love Jason

The best thing about having a MacBook Pro is that you can take it anywhere. Now I can have Jason time anytime:

On the patio with a cold one.

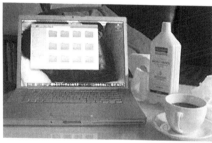

Over coffee.

Curling up in bed.

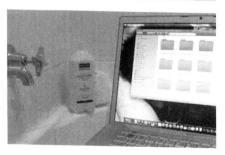

Or just relaxing in the bath.

# Camping With Simon

*Hello, my name is Simon and I love camping. I don't own any camping gear but this isn't problem as I've watched every series of Survivor. My favourite episode is the one where Jeff, the host, rode all the way from the Amazon on a jet ski to New York, crossing the Atlantic ocean, to read the votes in the final episode. This shows not only great dedication to fans, but also excellent seafaring and navigation skills.*

*Here's my step-by-step guide to camping with David:*

### Step 1

Ring David at 11pm and tell him you want to go camping the next day. Dictate a list of items you require him to prepare by the next morning, including tent and all supplies. If David asks any questions, become exasperated and explain to him that camping is about enjoying the great outdoors and each other's company, not about going halves for groceries and petrol money.

### Step 2

Ring David at 6.45am to add "Biscuits to eat on the trip" to the list.

## Step 3

Once David arrives to pick you up, read out the list and make David say the word 'check' after each item because that is how they do it on television and 'yep' is not a real word. Add pocket mirror to the list, berating David for not having the common sense to include this should you need to signal planes. Quote Lord Baden Powell's "Be prepared" a minimum of four times.

Before leaving, try on several combinations of cargo pants with baseball caps and consult David on the merits of each. If David states, "that looks fine", explain to him that you were just testing him and he failed, as you would never wear a green baseball cap with beige cargo pants out in public. If he mentions nobody else will be at the camp site to see the outfit, explain to him that you are taking a digital camera and will not be posting photos of yourself wearing a green baseball cap with beige cargo pants on Facebook.

## Step 4

Instruct David to take your bags out to the car while you check your email before leaving. Explain the importance of working together and good time management.

Once you have left, instruct David to pull into a service station to purchase AAA batteries and different biscuits to eat on the trip, as you only like the ones with cream in them. When David returns to the car, go into the service station to purchase biscuits yourself after stating it should have been obvious you did not mean Oreo's.

While inside, also purchase Billy Idol's greatest hits CD to listen to on the way because you like the track *Yell like a Rebel*.

## Step 5

During the four hour drive to the camp site, instruct David to pull over every thirty minutes so you can urinate behind a tree. It's important to do this when the only tree is several hundred metres away in a field. While urinating, peer around the tree at David sitting in the car. For the remainder of the drive, list words that lose all meaning when you say them fifty times such as 'yolk' and play the Billy Idol's greatest hits CD on loop while stating, "Oooh, I remember this one" at the beginning of each track.

Read out each road sign as you pass it. When it's a speed limit sign, lean across to glance at the speedometer.

## Step 6

Upon arrival, unpack a chair to sit on while David sets up camp. Point out what he could do to streamline the procedure. Instruct David to fetch your bag, as you did not realise the tent would be the same colour as your cargo pants and you wish to change. Explain that if you are photographed with the tent in the background it will look like you have no legs. Admonish David for purchasing AAA batteries when your digital camera takes AA. Inform David that AA and AAA are the correct terms and that only people who drive pickup trucks call them double and triple A.

## Step 7

Inform David that you are bored. If David suggests hiking or any other activity that requires leaving your chair, state that you are there to relax, not partake in extreme sports.

## Step 8

While David collects firewood, call out instructions regarding the size, type and density of wood required. As David is constructing the fire, point out the fundamental errors of his system and state that it is not the way you have seen it done on *Survivor*. Explain the teepee method of stick formation and its air circulation and flame consistency benefits. Once the fire is established, describe in detail how you prefer your sausages cooked, using pieces of bark as colour swatches to indicate the hue required. During dinner, calculate the ratio of burnt to unburnt sausage and evaluate David's ability to follow simple instructions at 17%. After dinner, state that it is a requirement while camping to sing songs around the campfire. When David declines, sing tracks from Billy Idol's greatest hits CD.

## Step 9

Declare that you are tired and wish to go to bed. If David replies that he will sit by the fire for a while, inform him that you are camping together and douse the fire with a bucket of water. Once in the tent, state that you always sleep naked and are not going to alter this just because you are camping. Wait until David is in his sleeping bag before requesting he retrieve your book from the car due to you being naked, not tired, and wishing to read for a while by torchlight. On his return, point out the fact that the torch is flat and that it takes AA batteries. Lay in the dark for several minutes before declaring that you are bored. Ask, "Did you hear that?" and, "Are you asleep?" every five minutes. Describe how uncomfortable you are, what you are missing on television, and hum tracks from Billy Idol's greatest hits CD.

## Step 10

Wake David at 1am and inform him of the protection and hunting benefits of making a bow and arrow. Take this opportunity to point out a small hole in the tent and ask David if he thinks it is large enough for spiders to get through. Describe in depth a television program you saw on Discovery channel about wasps laying eggs in spiders.

## Step 11

Wake David at 1.30am and ask if he thinks the hole is large enough for wasps to get through.

## Step 12

Wake David at 2am and tell him that you do not remember switching the iron off after ironing your cargo pants and that you are very concerned about the fact. Inform him that this will require cutting the camping trip short, packing up first thing in the morning and driving home. State that on the plus side, you just remembered the new series of 'V' starts tomorrow night on television and this means that you will not miss it. List science fiction shows from the seventies and eighties that you think should be redone for today's audience.

## Step 13

During the drive back, insinuate continuously that the Billy Idol CD has gone missing on purpose. State every half hour that you really felt like listening to it.

# Sponsor a
# Poor Black Boy

*He stinks and ate a rat with maggots today.*

*How would you like it?*

Bababada Didva Poor black boy

SEND
MONEY
NOW!

223

# Adelaide

*Roz Knorr - a pseudonym I assume unless she is part Klingon – doesn't like Adelaide. Or perhaps it's just me. She certainly doesn't like my website and seems to have missed the point that there are plenty of other blog posts discussing sweat shop children and how man has ravaged Mother Earth. Sometimes it is nice to have a pointless distraction. We can't spend every waking hour kissing grass and throwing paint at women wearing fur pants.*

**From:** Roz Knorr
**Date:** Monday 12 October 2009 11.56am
**To:** David Thorne
**Subject:** Adelaide loser

Only in a backwards town like Adelaide would you get dickheads who would write crap like you. You cant even write well. Thats the result of the sub standard backwards schools in Adelaide. Writing about monkeys and children starving. Spend a few nights with the Salvos feeding the homeless so you can write about that and at least people will go to your site and learn something loser. Little dick typical male. Face it when it comes to Adelaide it is full of dumb backwards hick arseholes that are totally devoid of social consciousness or culture.

**From:** David Thorne
**Date:** Monday 12 October 2009 12.38pm
**To:** Roz Knorr
**Subject:** Re: Adelaide loser

Dear Roz,

Thank you for your email. I apologise for the delay in replying - Adelaide is a tad behind other cities not only in regards to consciousness and culture, but also technology. Your email was received by Adelaide's only computer, a 386 housed in the public library powered by a duck on a treadmill, before being relayed to me by Morse code.

Should you wish to contact me directly next time, my home number is dot dot dash dot dash dot dot dash.

Regards, David

....................................................................................

**From:** Roz Knorr
**Date:** Tuesday 13 October 2009 9.18am
**To:** David Thorne
**Subject:** Re: Re: Adelaide loser

Your pathetic reply just shows what a backwards hick you are. I have homes in Hong Kong, Britain, Paris, USA, & Hawai, as well as Australia. I grew up in a house with 11 servants & a chaufer. And honey I have friends living in Laurel Canyon, & California who earn $400,000 a day in rock & roll.

Poor Adeliade. No culture and no class. Be careful not to be a victim of a hit & run. Accidents happen all the time, so much cheaper in Adelaide. One phone call...

**From:** David Thorne
**Date:** Tuesday 13 October 2009 9.51am
**To:** Roz Knorr
**Subject:** Re: Re: Re: Adelaide loser

Dear Roz,

Thank you for your concern and kind offer, but I should be fine for the moment in regards to monetary based injuries. I set up a stall at a women's golfing convention recently with a banner stating, "Punch me in the head for one dollar." I made eight hundred and thirty dollars that day. With the money raised, I intend to buy a bigger stall for next year's convention.

Contrary to your statement regarding Adelaide having no culture, there is actually a large and thriving artistic community here. Unfortunately, very little art is produced due mainly to the artists spending all their time displaying their scarves to each other and attending gallery exhibitions for the free alcohol, food, and the chance to wash their armpits in the venue's bathroom.

Regards, David

........................................................................................

**From:** Roz Knorr
**Date:** Tuesday 13 October 2009 2.14pm
**To:** David Thorne
**Subject:** Re: Re: Re: Re: Adelaide loser

You wouldn't know a thing about culture being from Adelaide. You're a bunch of inbred filthy convicts and no hoppers. I won't even quote you how much money I make from my businesses that I have in New York, Britain or Japan..

**From:** David Thorne
**Date:** Tuesday 13 October 2009 3.02pm
**To:** Roz Knorr
**Subject:** Re: Re: Re: Re: Re: Adelaide loser

Dear Roz,

Actually, while Adelaide may commonly be referred to as the murder capital of Australia due to having more serial killers per capita than any other city in Australia, it's ironically the only Australian capital city not founded by convicts. Adelaide is also known as the City of Churches due to the fact that there is a church on every corner. It's not surprising therefore that Adelaide also has a long history of child pedophilia. Another common misconception is that due to Adelaide's high number of churches, the city must be a very religious one. In fact, the number of churches is only necessary in order to cope with the number of funerals as a result of the number of murders that take place here.

You are also mistaken in regards to Adelaide containing no hoppers. I myself regularly hop. I am, in fact, the founder of the Adelaide Hopping Club, an organisation that meets each Tuesday to hop. We have so many members that it is often standing room only at the meetings. Which is obviously not a problem.

Recently, we have been planning an event in which we intend to hop non stop from Adelaide to Sydney to raise not only awareness for the sport of hopping but also funds for a new charity we have set up called The Roz Knorr Hopping Foundation which will provide poor people with no legs a single artificial leg and accompanying hopping instructional video inspiringly titled *Never Give Up Hop*.

Regards, David

**From:** Roz Knorr
**Date:** Wednesday 14 October 2009 11.16am
**To:** David Thorne
**Subject:** Re: Re: Re: Re: Re: Re: Adelaide loser

You wouldn't know the first thing about charity or giving back to the community. People from Adelaide don't do anything for the underprivileged in society. Go read Naomi Klein's 1999 book "No Logo" and join the ant-globalist movement & start defacing corporate posters in public places with political statements, or visit a sweat shop with 7 year olds in Mexico & blog about it. Until then you are just another selfish parasite taking from this planet.

Watch your back. I leave for New York in my private plain this afternoon so I don't have any time for anymore of your pathetic hick town nonsense.

Goodbye David.

........................................................................................

**From:** David Thorne
**Date:** Thursday 15 October 2009 11.55am
**To:** Roz Knorr
**Subject:** Re: Re: Re: Re: Re: Re: Re: Adelaide loser

Dear Roz,

Thank you for the excellent suggestions. Unfortunately I cannot afford the airfare to Mexico and even if I did, I do not know any seven year olds to take. It's a pity as I've heard you can get cheap soccer balls there.

Coincidentally, I too have a private plain. It's actually more of a field but going by the amount of backpackers discovered buried there, quite private regardless.

I was sitting in the middle of it reading your correspondence regarding poorly written books and stale political statements, when I realised you raise a valid point. I therefore intend to organise a garage sale, sell my neighbours outdoor furniture, and use the proceeds to move to Nimbin where I'll spent my days rubbing my body with crystals, dancing to Fleetwood Mac, and braiding my leg hair to form rope which I will use to construct dream catchers to sell at the local commune shop.

Regards, David

....................................................................................

**From:** Roz Knorr
**Date:** Friday 16 October 2009 10.41am
**To:** David Thorne
**Subject:** Re: Re: Re: Re: Re: Re: Re: Re: Adelaide loser

Dangerous ground loser. You do not know whom you are dealing with. I know a lot of people.

....................................................................................

**From:** David Thorne
**Date:** Friday 16 October 2009 11.09am
**To:** Roz Knorr
**Subject:** Re: Re: Re: Re: Re: Re: Re: Re: Re: Adelaide loser

Dear Roz,

Yes, I calculate the six real estate agents, pilot and co-pilot of your private plain, your rock and roll friends making $400,000 a day, plus the eleven servants and chauffeur, makes a total of twenty-two.

I'm assuming the chauffeur is the person you intend to have me run over by, if not, then twenty-three.

This total does not of course include the people you know from the Salvation Army, anti-globalist movements, sweat shop owners, the shop assistant at your local XXL Golf Pants'R'Us, or members of the K.D. Lang Fan Club.

Regards, David

⋯⋯⋯⋯⋯⋯⋯⋯⋯⋯⋯⋯⋯⋯⋯⋯⋯⋯⋯⋯⋯⋯⋯⋯⋯⋯⋯⋯⋯⋯

**From:** Roz Knorr
**Date:** Friday 16 October 2009 2.01pm
**To:** David Thorne
**Subject:** Re: Re: Re: Re: Re: Re: Re: Re: Re: Re: Adelaide loser

Email me agian and you will be sorry. Bye.

⋯⋯⋯⋯⋯⋯⋯⋯⋯⋯⋯⋯⋯⋯⋯⋯⋯⋯⋯⋯⋯⋯⋯⋯⋯⋯⋯⋯⋯⋯

**From:** David Thorne
**Date:** Friday 16 October 2009 2.07pm
**To:** Roz Knorr
**Subject:** Re: Re: Re: Re: Re: Re: Re: Re: Re: Re: Re: Adelaide loser

■ •• ■ • ■ ■ •

# Hello, my name is Holly and I love playing tennis.

*Not with David though because he cheats. Once, while we were watching Jeopardy, he forgot to say, "What is..." before answering the question but gave himself a point anyway. What's wrong with some people? It isn't that hard – Alex gives you the answer and you answer with the question. Playing by the rules makes it more fun for everyone. Play it properly or go watch the televisoin in the bedroom. I don't care if it hasn't got cable, it has the local channels. It's your choice.*

### Introduction to Tennis

Considered by some as a game and others as the terrifying act of exercising by choice, tennis, invented in 1976, involves fun things to do with racquets and balls. You can swing a racquet. You can hit a ball. Tennis is also an exciting spectator sport which allows people to watch other people swing racquets and hit balls.

Each game lasts for approximately four hours. Three hours of this consists of picking up the balls so that you can hit them again with a racquet. The remaining hour is spent arguing.

## Scoring

There are only four basic rules to scoring:

**1.** If David hits the shot in, then it is out and you get a point.
**2.** If David hits it out, then you get a point.
**3.** If at any point David asks what the score is, his inability to pay attention means you get three points.
**4.** Hitting balls over the fence gives you a few minutes to relax while David collects them and two points.

A standard scoring sequence consists of "Fifteen love, fifteen all, forty love, I win." It would make more sense to just make it the first to four but the game was invented by the British who only discovered consecutive numeric sequencing following the 1982 release of XTC's single *Senses Working Overtime*.

If David questions the accuracy of the score, this means he is cheating. Display disappointment at his inability to be trusted and point out that you should be used to his lies because of the time he told you the movie *28 Weeks Later* was a romantic comedy.

## Racquet Selection

It doesn't matter what brand or quality the racquet is, as long as it's pink. It's preferable that the racquet is not a recognised brand as this enables you to blame any lost points on it. Reiterate this to David by throwing the racquet in disgust several times per match and, when failing to return a shot, stare at the racquet with a look of disdain as if to say, "What the fuck racquet? What are you doing? That wouldn't have happened if you were the kind of racquet Andre Agassi uses."

After winning a point, declare that not only was it a point won, it was a point won with inferior equipment.

### Clothing

Before each game, it is imperative to purchase a new outfit. If David cannot locate his tennis shorts, suggest he wear his yellow swimming trunks with the palm trees and starfish on them because it's just a game of tennis, nobody will be there to see him, and he's not Andre Agassi.

### Preparation

Prior to each game, an injury should be prepared. It does not need to be dependant on the outcome as *You only won the game because of my possibly broken leg* works just as well as *I won despite my possibly broken leg.*

### Serving

Every serve David makes is out. Being closer to the area that the ball was meant to be hit into means your view is the only one that can be trusted and he just thought it was in because he is "looking at it from further away and on the wrong angle."

All serves you make are in for exactly the same reason. If David mentions that you are not wearing your glasses, state that your vision is clear enough to see through his lies.

### Obstruction

Obstruction is an integral component of every tennis match. If David serves a ball that you simply cannot be bothered attempting to reach, calling out "obstruction" means the shot is void and must be made again. It doesn't matter what the obstruction is, a stick nearby or a dog that you saw on the side of the road the previous day while driving to work will do. If David questions the validity of this rule, remind him that it is just a game and he's not Andre Agassi.

## Game Play

A winning shot should be accompanied by a small dance and admonishment if David does not agree the shot was possibly the greatest shot ever made in the history of tennis. A winning shot by David should be met with the statement, "The sun was in my eyes" or, "Nobody likes you, you do realise that don't you?" and a look such as the one you use when you ask him to drive to the shop to get sour cream for nachos and he comes back with a twelve pack of Bic lighters and a folding chair.

If you are losing the game, it is important that David realises it is not because he is playing well, it is because you don't care.

Standard procedures include:

**1.** Hang on, David's serving, I'll put you on hold for a second.

**2.** Yes, I'm ready. Go ahead and serve.

**3.** Fuck this; I'm going home to watch *Jeopardy*.

## Game, Set, Match

If you have won the match, request another. If you have lost (due to the racquet not being the kind Andre Agassi uses and your leg hurting), do not speak to David on the drive home. Play a Dixie Chicks CD.

# Jumping Frog Fee

*There are many things to be said for working in the design industry but as they are mostly negative, especially those regarding clients, I'd rather write about robots. If I were a robot, programmed to serve people all day, I'd throw myself off a cliff. Working in the design industry is a lot like being a robot. A robot that curses its positronic brain for not allowing it to ignore the first law and attach spinning blades to its arms and take out the next client that states, "that's nice but can we try it in green?" or, "Can you make the text bigger?"*

*Actually, scratch that, working in the design industry is more like being a whore. A dirty whore who has programmed their mind to find a happy place rather than be outraged by client requests. There are many things to be said for working in the design industry but mostly that it is like being a dirty robot whore.*

**From:** Robert Schaefer
**Date:** Monday 8 November 2010 9.11am
**To:** David Thorne
**Subject:** Artwork

Hello David,

Can you send me the artwork for our business cards you did

last year. Finsbury Press has asked for the original files. I need the artwork before Wednesday so either this afternoon or tomorrow is fine.

Thanks Rob

........................................................................................

**From:** David Thorne
**Date:** Monday 8 November 2010 10.24am
**To:** Robert Schaefer
**Subject:** Re: Artwork

Hello Bob,

I no longer work for that agency. Due to client account management resembling that German dance where men in tights slap each other, the company was basically trading insolvent and I resigned. While some may see this as the proverbial rat deserting a sinking ship, I prefer to think of it as quietly stepping out of a bathtub you have been sharing with four retarded children while they are busy arguing over who lost the soap.

I'd suggest contacting the agency and requesting your business card artwork before the owner swaps the art department computers for magic beans.

Alternatively, if you would like me to recreate the files for you, I'd be happy to help. I estimate this would take three hours at seventy-five dollars per hour.

Regards, David

**From:** Robert Schaefer
**Date:** Monday 8 November 2010 12.17pm
**To:** David Thorne
**Subject:** Re: Re: Artwork

It's Rob not Bob and I already emailed them and they said they don't have the files and to contact you. I'm not paying you $225 for artwork when I already paid you for the artwork last year.

---

**From:** David Thorne
**Date:** Monday 8 November 2010 3.02pm
**To:** Robert Schaefer
**Subject:** Re: Re: Re: Artwork

Dear Bob,

You paid the agency to provide artwork and I no longer work for that agency. While generally a frontline supporter of questioning logic, this support wavers drastically in the face of providing free work.

A few years back, I bought my first four-wheel-drive vehicle. The salesman who did the paperwork was named Roger. While on a camping trip several months later with my offspring, I parked the vehicle on a dirt incline near a river and set up camp. We awoke the next morning to discover it had rained, turning the dirt incline into a slippery mud incline, and our vehicle had slid roof-deep into the river. Realising my phone was on the rear seat of the vehicle, along with our food, we rode a Coleman® inflatable air mattress down the river to the nearest town. It was a full days' journey and I will admit the thought of eating my offspring crossed my mind.

This was less due to hunger than his constant complaining of, "Why do I have to hold on to the back while you ride?" and, "I can't feel my legs."

My offspring and I went shopping for a new vehicle a few weeks later. I did not to turn up at Roger's premises demanding a replacement vehicle for the one I lost. While it's possible Roger may have nodded, sympathized, and explained patiently the structure of modern commerce, it's more likely he would have just called me a dickhead.

Also, while three hours at $75.00 does equate to $225.00, the total cost to recreate and sent your business card artwork would be $450.00 due to the Jumping Frog fee.

Regards, David

..................................................................................................

**From:** Robert Schaefer
**Date:** Monday 8 November 2010 3.18pm
**To:** David Thorne
**Subject:** Re: Re: Re: Re: Artwork

I remember you from the meeting you were that idiot wearing a green Atari t-shirt.

Im NOT paying for work I have already paid for and 3 hours at $75.00 per hour is $225.00 NOT $450.00 - that is double. where the did you get double from and what the fuck is a jumping frog fee?

**From:** David Thorne
**Date:** Monday 8 November 2010 4.46pm
**To:** Robert Schaefer
**Subject:** Re: Re: Re: Re: Re: Artwork

Dear Bob,

I remember you from the meeting too (specifically your haggling over price and questioning why animated gifs can't be used on your business card) but no, sadly the Atari clad individual would have been Thomas, the owner. Nearing fifty, he feels retro t-shirts and trucker caps like the cool kids wear, disguise the fact. Once you've seen his size 40 lower-half squeezed into size 32 skinny jeans, like two parallel overflowing cake icing funnels, it can never be unseen.

I would have been the idiot wearing a suit and feigning interest in your business card requirements by appearing to take notes but actually creating an itemised list of things I would rather be doing, starting with #1. Being shot in the neck with an arrow.

Sometimes when I'm in meetings, I imagine I'm a robot programmed not to realise I am a robot and if the code word 'quantifiable' is mentioned, I will explode. Other times, I imagine I am a small Indian girl collecting water for my village in a brightly painted clay pot.

The Jumping Frog fee relates to an event early on in my career when I made the mistake of offering a client a fixed price for a two-hundred-page website. Once the design was signed off and the build completed over a three-month period, the client requested that each page include a frog jumping around the screen because his wife liked frogs.

Purchasing a frog from the local pet store and filming it by holding a camera above and prodding it to jump, I spent the next two weeks incorporating it into every page of the website.

A few days later, the client described the addition as, "Very annoying," and requested it be removed and replaced with a 3D animated frog jumping onto the screen, holding a thumb up, and speaking the words, "Jump on down and grab a bargain."

After providing a quote for this, I was informed that the amendments would be made "under the original fixed price or no payment would be made at all." The next day, their home page was replaced with a single image of a frog giving the finger and a voice bubble stating, "I jump for cash, bitch."

After fifteen years in the design industry, I've realised the only difference between sitting in front of a computer facilitating client's requests and kneeling on a urine soaked truck-stop bathroom floor giving five dollar blowjobs to men named Chuck, is the amount of urine on the floor. As such, the Jumping Frog fee has evolved from insurance against post-project client demands, to client incentive to have somebody else do it.

Regards, David

....................................................................................

**From:** Robert Schaefer
**Date:** Monday 8 November 2010 5.09pm
**To:** David Thorne
**Subject:** Re: Re: Re: Re: Re: Re: Artwork

You have until 10am tomorrow morning to send me the business card artwork or you will hear from my lawyer. I'm sick to death of dealing with you designers. Being able to draw and dressing like women doesn't make you special. You've got no idea who you're dealing with.

**From:** David Thorne
**Date:** Monday 8 November 2010 5.37pm
**To:** Robert Schaefer
**Subject:** Re: Re: Re: Re: Re: Re: Re: Artwork

Dear Bobupanddown,

That may be so but the label, "Some dick who wants free shit", doesn't require CSI profiling and while I am no lawyer, I question testimony comprising of, "I paid an agency to provide me files, I lost the files, I now demand some guy who used to work there give me new files," would have much legal standing.

I also question your dissatisfaction with the price I have quoted as I believe the original charge for your work by the agency was around fifteen-hundred-dollars. While the actual process would have consisted of ten minutes on iStock.com for the background, two minutes pretending to consider a typeface other than Helvetica, and ten minutes putting it together, this is standard design industry practice and listed under 'Direction, Design and Build' on the invoice.

I do understand your objection to the established system of exchange of money for services though; I personally envision a utopian future where cash is replaced with interpretive dance. We agree on a particular style that seeks to translate particular feelings and emotions into movement and dramatic expression in exchange for groceries or business card artwork. And we all own jetpacks.

In a moment of stupidity, I once agreed to design and built a website in exchange for yoga lessons. Contrary to what they would have you believe, you cannot actually embrace the sun as this would result in severe burns and your arms would need to be over one hundred and fifty million miles long. My favourite yoga move is the wriggly snake.

Unfortunately, until I can pay rent with mantras or grand eloquent movements in Spandex, I'll need cash.

Regards, David.

......................................................................................

**From:** Robert Schaefer
**Date:** Monday 8 November 2010 5.44pm
**To:** David Thorne
**Subject:** Re: Re: Re: Re: Re: Re: Re: Re: Artwork

Fine. Send me the completed business card artwork tonight with an invoice.

......................................................................................

**From:** David Thorne
**Date:** Monday 8 November 2010 5.49pm
**To:** Robert Schaefer
**Subject:** File attached:

# Magic 8 Ball

*I sent an email to a friend recently, asking several different questions, and he replied with the single answer "Yes, probably." Obviously he had either not bothered reading the email or could not be bothered answering my questions. The next day, I replied to emails using a Mattel® Magic 8 Ball to generate answers.*

**From:** Simon
**Date:** Wednesday 4 Feb 2009 9.38am
**To:** David Thorne
**Subject:** No Subject

Have you got a typeface called Garamond Semibold? I have the Garamond and bold and italic but not the semibold. I'm doing a poster for Cathy and I reckon garamond would look good.

...................................................................................................

**From:** David Thorne
**Date:** Wednesday 4 Feb 2009 10.02am
**To:** Simon
**Subject:** Re: No Subject

As I see it, yes.

**From:** Simon
**Date:** Wednesday 4 Feb 2009 10.43am
**To:** David Thorne
**Subject:** Garamond

Which one? Yes you have the typeface or that it would look good on a poster?

**From:** David Thorne
**Date:** Wednesday 4 Feb 2009 10.52am
**To:** Simon
**Subject:** Re: Garamond

Concentrate and ask again.

**From:** Simon
**Date:** Wednesday 4 Feb 2009 11.14am
**To:** David Thorne
**Subject:** Re: Re: Garamond

What the fuck? I need the typeface Garamond. Have you got it or not?

**From:** David Thorne
**Date:** Wednesday 4 Feb 2009 11.18am
**To:** Simon
**Subject:** Re: Re: Re: Garamond

You may rely on it.

**From:** Simon
**Date:** Wednesday 4 Feb 2009 11.29am
**To:** David Thorne
**Subject:** Re: Re: Re: Re: Garamond

Send me the typeface dickhead.

.......................................................................................

**From:** Mark Pierce
**Date:** Wednesday 4 Feb 2009 2.08pm
**To:** David Thorne
**Subject:** Hey

Hey. Are you at work?

.......................................................................................

**From:** David Thorne
**Date:** Wednesday 4 Feb 2009 2.25pm
**To:** Mark Pierce
**Subject:** Re: Hey

Signs point to yes.

.......................................................................................

**From:** Mark Pierce
**Date:** Wednesday 4 Feb 2009 2.53pm
**To:** David Thorne
**Subject:** Re: Re: Hey

What signs? Can you drop over on your way home from work
and help me move my desk into the spare room? The glass top
is too heavy to lift.

**From:** David Thorne
**Date:** Wednesday 4 Feb 2009 3.22pm
**To:** Mark Pierce
**Subject:** Re: Re: Re: Hey

My sources say no.

........................................................................................

**From:** Mark Pierce
**Date:** Wednesday 4 Feb 2009 3.49pm
**To:** David Thorne
**Subject:** Re: Re: Re: Re: Hey

Are you serious? I tried lifting it a bit at a time and sliding it but
I need help. Can you come for a quick drive now?

........................................................................................

**From:** David Thorne
**Date:** Wednesday 4 Feb 2009 4.02pm
**To:** Mark Pierce
**Subject:** Re: Re: Re: Re: Re: Hey

Ask again later.

........................................................................................

**From:** Mark Pierce
**Date:** Wednesday 4 Feb 2009 4.57pm
**To:** David Thorne
**Subject:** ?

Are you going to help me after work or not?

**From:** David Thorne
**Date:** Wednesday 4 Feb 2009 5.16pm
**To:** Mark Pierce
**Subject:** Re: ?

It is decidedly so.

---

**From:** Mark Pierce
**Date:** Wednesday 4 Feb 2009 5.24pm
**To:** David Thorne
**Subject:** Re: Re: ?

Good. Fuck you are annoying sometimes.

---

**From:** Justine Murphy
**Date:** Wednesday 4 Feb 2009 8.14pm
**To:** David Thorne
**Subject:** Tree frogs ppt

Hi David, you forgot to send the attachment on your last email. Can you send it again please?

Justine

---

**From:** David Thorne
**Date:** Wednesday 4 Feb 2009 8.51pm
**To:** Justine Murphy
**Subject:** Re: Tree frogs ppt

You may rely on it.

**From:** Justine Murphy
**Date:** Wednesday 4 Feb 2009 9.15pm
**To:** David Thorne
**Subject:** Re: Re: Tree frogs ppt

Ok. Can you resend it to me then please?

........................................................................................................

**From:** David Thorne
**Date:** Wednesday 4 Feb 2009 9.26pm
**To:** Justine Murphy
**Subject:** Re: Re: Re: Tree frogs ppt

Without a doubt.

........................................................................................................

**From:** Justine Murphy
**Date:** Wednesday 4 Feb 2009 9.44pm
**To:** David Thorne
**Subject:** Re: Re: Re: Re: Tree frogs ppt

???? Did you attach it?

........................................................................................................

**From:** David Thorne
**Date:** Wednesday 4 Feb 2009 9.51pm
**To:** Justine Murphy
**Subject:** Re: Re: Re: Re: Re: Tree frogs ppt

Don't count on it.

**From:** Justine Murphy
**Date:** Wednesday 4 Feb 2009 10.27pm
**To:** David Thorne
**Subject:** Re: Re: Re: Re: Re: Re: Tree frogs ppt

Just attachment it asshat.

.......................................................................................

**From:** Simon
**Date:** Wednesday 4 Feb 2009 11.28pm
**To:** David Thorne
**Subject:** No Subject

Are you online?

.......................................................................................

**From:** David Thorne
**Date:** Wednesday 4 Feb 2009 11.37pm
**To:** Simon
**Subject:** Re: No Subject

Concentrate and ask again.

.......................................................................................

**From:** Simon
**Date:** Wednesday 4 Feb 2009 11.41pm
**To:** David Thorne
**Subject:** Re: Re: No Subject

Fuck you.

# About the Author

David Thorne works in the design and branding industry, as he is too lazy and easily distracted to do a real job. Amongst the multitude of his qualities, which include reciting prime numbers backwards from 909526, reading to blind children and training guide dogs, embellishment may be at the top.

David currently resides with his partner Holly (who recently made the top 100 on *So You Think You Can Dance*), in the small village of Harrisonburg, Virginia, having escaped from Adelaide, South Australia in 2010. He was born in Geraldton, Western Australia to Welsh immigrant parents and has an older sister who once attempted to set his bedroom alight with him locked inside. Police did not press charges.

He has worked as a horse riding instructor, bartender, Apple design system consultant, graphic designer, copywriter, branding consultant, and design director, and describes working in the design industry as, "The most uncreative experience of my life."

He stays up too late, drinks too much coffee, smokes too much, hates getting up in the morning, and has offspring who thinks David doesn't know what he has been up to when he deletes his Internet history.